Learning and Teaching in
Social Work

Learning and Teaching in Social Work Practice

Audrey Beverley
and
Aidan Worsley

First published in 2007 by
PALGRAVE MACMILLAN
Houndmills, Basingstoke, Hampshire RG21 6XS and
175 Fifth Avenue, New York, N.Y. 10010
Companies and representatives throughout the world.

PALGRAVE MACMILLAN is the global academic imprint of the Palgrave Macmillan division of St. Martin's Press, LLC and of Palgrave Macmillan Ltd. Macmillan® is a registered trademark in the United States, United Kingdom and other countries. Palgrave is a registered trademark in the European Union and other countries.

ISBN-13: 978–1–4039–9414–1
ISBN-10: 1–4039–9414–5

This book is printed on paper suitable for recycling and made from fully managed and sustained forest sources. Logging, pulping and manufacturing processes are expected to conform to the environmental regulations of the country of origin.

A catalogue record for this book is available from the British Library.

A catalog record for this book is available from the Library of Congress.

I would like to dedicate this book to the memory of my beautiful daughter Faith. Her experience as a learner on placement was in part an inspiration for writing a book to assist enablers in their tasks. Tragically Faith died after a battle with cancer during the production of the book and never saw it finished.

Audrey Beverley

This book is dedicated to my wife, Lesley, and daughter, Rhiannon for their patience and love.

Aidan Worsley

Contents

List of Diagrams

Preface

Those working within social work as learners or enablers will be familiar with the contention that change is one of the characteristics of the professional arena. Some might go further and agree with the social reformer Havelock Ellis (1859–1939) who considered that progress was the exchange of one nuisance for another. All workers within social work have a responsibility to ensure that they are as up-to-date as possible in matters of policy, procedure, service delivery, research and the general development of practice within their particular professional and regional setting. This book, aimed at workers in this wide variety of fields, must acknowledge that learning and enabling takes place within a constantly shifting context of social policy. To that end, we offer a list of helpful Web-based resources that the reader may find useful in ensuring that their learning and enabling are at the forefront of current debate.

Care Councils

http://www.ccwales.org.uk/
Cyngor Gofal Cymru/Care Council for Wales

http://www.gscc.org.uk/Home/
General Social Care Council (England)

http://www.niscc.info/
Northern Ireland Social Care Council

http://www.sssc.uk.com/Homepage.htm
Scottish Social Services Council

Skills Councils

http://www.cwdcouncil.org.uk/
Children's Workforce Development Council

http://www.lsc.gov.uk/
Learning and Skills Council (England)

http://www.skillsforcare.org.uk/
Skills for Care (England)

http://www.skillsforcareanddevelopment.org.uk/view.aspx?id=15
Skills for Care and Development (UK)

http://www.skillsforhealth.org.uk/
Skills for Health

http://www.skillsforjustice.com/default.asp?PageID=1
Skills for Justice

Relevant General Sites

http://www.adss.org.uk/
Association of Directors of Social Services

http://www.basw.co.uk/index.php
British Association of Social Workers

http://www.communitycare.co.uk/Home/Default.aspx
Community Care

http://www.dfes.gov.uk/
Department of Education and Skills

http://www.dh.gov.uk/Home/fs/en
Department of Health

http://www.intute.ac.uk/socialsciences/
Intute Social Sciences Guide to Web based resources

http://www.nopt.org/
National Organisation for Practice Teaching

http://www.qaa.org.uk/
Quality Assurance Agency for Higher Education

http://www.resmind.swap.ac.uk/
Research Mindedness in Social Work and Social Care

http://www.scie.org.uk/
Social Care Institute for Excellence

http://www.swap.ac.uk/
Social Policy and Social Work subject centre of Higher Education Academy

Introduction

As the social care workforce grows in number and variety, the expectations placed upon it seem to increase proportionately. Continuing professional development assumes particular significance in such a scenario: how can staff develop the knowledge and skills required to respond to the dynamics of social care and how can they continue to do so throughout their careers? Such achievement cannot be left to chance and personal inclination – surely the needs of service users underlines that point. It seems that what is required is a planned and structured approach to professional development in social care. This book is a contribution to that approach.

If you are involved in the teaching and assessment of practice within the social work or social care environment, this book is for you. If you are learning within this setting, this book will also prove invaluable. The roles of 'learner' and 'enabler' find many different expressions within social work practice, and this book is designed to meet their needs. You may be a student on pre-qualifying, qualifying or post-qualifying social work education programmes or just someone wanting to extend his or her knowledge and skills. You may be the person who facilitates that learning. You could have any one of a number of titles including work-based assessor, practice teacher, mentor, practice assessor, practice supervisor, staff development officer, human resource manager, line manager and possibly many others. Academic staff involved in a whole range of social work/care education may also find the content helpful. Whatever your title, this book is for those who have a role in the education, training and development of others in their workplace.

The Code of Practice for social care employees requires *all* workers to 'contribute to the learning and development of others' (GSCC, 2002). In this sense this is a book for everyone who works or wishes to work in social care – across the statutory, private, voluntary and independent sectors – and across the national boundaries of the United Kingdom. All the countries in the United Kingdom have considered the future of their social care workforces with some producing far-reaching recommendations that may impact on professional education and development (see, for example, DOH, 2006; Drakeford, 2006; Scottish Executive, 2006; Welsh Assembly, 2006). Wherever we work, the development of the workforce is the business of all within that workforce and the differing experiences of workers within the United Kingdom should not mask the essentially congruent nature of learning and enabling in the workplace across these boundaries. We believe there remains an essential similarity in the development of learning and enabling in the workplace across the United Kingdom.

It is not intended that this book should be read from cover to cover (although it certainly can be); readers are encouraged to select the chapters that are most appropriate to them at their particular point in the learning or teaching process. We firmly hold to the belief that learning is a lifelong process and learning by doing is an effective strategy. The concept of 'learning to learn' is fundamental to the book and we hope that it will help busy people to develop the skills needed to set them up as lifelong learners. Those readers who have a theoretical approach to learning may well wish to take their reading further and look to the original sources of much of the information gathered in the book. Where relevant, we have placed the topic for each chapter in a broader social policy context. We have included underpinning knowledge on each topic either from theory, research or practice wisdom gathered from working with a range of learners and enablers. Each chapter also includes a range of practical activities that we hope will allow the reader to see how concepts can be translated into practice. The activities can also be useful in extending the repertoire of learning methods utilised by learners and enablers alike. Some of the ideas and concepts appear in more than one chapter to help the reader who is picking out those areas most pertinent to him or her.

The book loosely mirrors the typical life course of a learning partnership in its structure. Chapter 1 will set the scene for learning and assessing in the social work/care workforce, considering the reality of learning environments and the organisations in which they are located. Chapter 2 is concerned with the learning partnership between learner and enabler – the core of any learning situation. Consideration is given to the different styles of learning partnership which reflect both the varied types of partnerships needed in different situations and the different aspects of power involved. Chapter 3 is concerned with how adults learn. It includes a range of different theoretical ideas about learning and suggestions as to how these ideas can be incorporated into practice. Central to the chapter is making learning as easy as possible by tailoring it to the individuality of each learner. The link between learning styles and enabler styles is explored in order to circumvent difficulties in the learning relationship. Chapter 4 is about creating and using learning opportunities. With a range of settings being used for practice in social work across a variety of different agencies, it is necessary to ensure that learners are provided with appropriate opportunities to enable them to learn. Chapter 5 is about the process of supervision which is the vehicle used to bring all parts of learning together. The chapter is concerned with encouraging the participants in the supervisory relationship to develop a shared view of the purpose and process of supervision. Chapter 6 is about reflective practice. Some of the literature on reflective practice is considered, and exercises are included to help both learner and enabler develop their skills in this important area and to stimulate the connections between theory and practice. The chapter concludes with a discussion on the nature of reflection and professional identity. Chapter 7 is concerned with evidencing and assessing competence. This chapter considers some of the history of competence-based assessment and tries to identify ideas which overcome some of the mechanical aspects of this construct. It covers the literature on the purposes and principles of assessment. Chapter 8 is concerned with learning in a multidisciplinary setting. This chapter covers the inclusion of people from other professions within the learning relationship, and gives ideas about breaking down barriers and capitalising on the advantages available from this situation. Models for effective working are considered. Chapter 9 deals with difficulties in the learning relationship. This chapter explores some of the challenges in the learning partnership and makes some suggestions on how to prevent them from occurring and how to deal with them when they have occurred. It deals with circumstances when performance is not competent, including identifying concerns and making recommendations.

We will argue that many of the developments in social work lead us to see a widening of areas where learning will take place and an ongoing, developing role for people who can enable others in the workplace. We both started our enabling careers as social workers working with students on qualifying courses. Since then our enabling roles have expanded into different areas. We have found the knowledge and skills acquired during practice teacher training and subsequent practice invaluable, but we have seen it adapted, extended and changed according to the different roles we have undertaken. We wanted to use our experiences to write a book which would be useful for learners and facilitators working across a broad learning continuum. The idea for this book came from ongoing discussions between the two authors about the implications for work-based learning from the developments of the social work degree and the post-qualifying training framework for social workers. Both authors have been involved for many years in practice teaching as practitioners and as managers of regional Practice Teacher Training Programmes. Both authors have been committee members and co-chairs of the National Organisation for Practice Teaching (NOPT) which is committed to quality in practice learning.

CHAPTER 1

Setting the Context for Learning

Social Work Education

The social work/care sector workforce has yet to emerge from a persistent modernising process that has characterised its recent years and continues to bring about significant change. This chapter will provide an overview of some of the changes in social work education before looking more broadly at concepts such as the 'learning organisation' and the management of change within social work. One transition that perhaps underpins all others is the introduction of the social care register. Everyone who works in social care will be required to join the register and abide by the Codes of Practice for Employees. The Code of Practice for Employers governs the agencies in which they work. The title 'social worker' is legally protected (since1 April 2005) so that only those who are properly qualified, registered and accountable will be able to use that title. The Codes of Practice are a critical part of regulating the social care workforce. All those registered would have agreed to abide by the Code, which contains criteria to guide practice and standards of conduct which workers have to meet across the four countries and their care councils (Care Council for Wales, General Social Care Council (GSCC), Northern Ireland Social Care Council and the Scottish Social Services Council – see the preface for Web links to these organisations). Employers will know what part they are expected to play in the regulation of the workforce and the support of high -quality social care. Service users and members of the public will be able to use the Codes to understand how a social care worker should behave towards them (GSCC, 2002).

The Code of Practice for Employees includes a requirement that social care workers are responsible for maintaining and improving their knowledge and skills. This should include undertaking relevant training towards professional development as well as their contribution to the learning and development of others (Requirement 6). There is a matching requirement in the Code for Employers (Requirement 3) which states that employers must provide training and development opportunities to enable social care workers to strengthen and develop their skills and knowledge. In order to do this they should do the following (GSCC, 2002).

- Provide induction, training and development opportunities to help staff do their jobs effectively and prepare for new roles and responsibilities.
- Contribute to the provision of social care and social work education and training including *effective workplace assessment and practice learning* (italics added).
- Support staff in posts subject to registration to meet GSCC's eligibility criteria for registration and it's requirements for continuing professional development.
- Respond appropriately to social care workers who seek assistance because they do not feel able or adequately prepared to carry out aspects of their work.

Clearly, there is now a strong emphasis on ensuring that the social work/care workforce is equipped to do its job by providing the education and training for each job role and ensuring that workers continue to learn and develop. Current government thinking for both the childcare and adult social care workforce (DOH, 2003, 2005) includes the idea that all staff should have personal development plans which identify learning and development needs and ways in which these needs will be met. Employers are expected to deploy a significant percentage of their staff-training budget on workforce development and individual employees are expected to contribute to the cost of their own development. Statutory inspectors will consider all these factors, and the progress made will have significant impact on the 'star ratings' of employers.

Continual professional development is implicit in personal development planning. Continuation as a registered social worker will be dependent on demonstration of 15 days of professional development over the three years of registration. However, the criteria for what constitutes professional development are somewhat vague and do not necessarily include any assessment about the impact of that development on practice. A revised framework for Post Qualifying (PQ) awards was agreed in September 2004 and has been available since September 2006. The framework does not currently connect with the continuing professional development requirements of registration. We would argue that the incentive for agencies to support staff on formal PQ awards when they are not required to do so by statute or target is severely compromised. Agencies *are* required to support all their registered social workers over each three-year period to undertake 15 days of professional development. PQ awards are likely to entail considerably more time than this, and the expense involved may lead employers to use other routes for their staff to meet the requirements. We would argue that a stronger and more cohesive system would integrate these strands of learning.

The social work degree that produced its first graduates in 2006 has a greater number of days of assessed practice than the previous DipSW programmes, increasing from 120 to 200 days on the degree. A wider range of practice learning opportunities is needed to meet this demand. Practice learning opportunities are being created in agencies that have traditionally not taken social work students and a variety of new ways of offering practice learning opportunities are being developed (Doel, 2005). Students on the degree can expect to undertake practice in more than one unit, delivering services during any single practice learning opportunity. As services become more specialised and more widespread it is less common for them to be able to provide all learning opportunities needed under one roof. Networks of opportunities are now being created, and although they provide a rich source of learning they need careful management to be effective.

When details of the social work degree were published, some were concerned that the role of the practice teacher had disappeared and been replaced by a new creature, the 'practice assessor'. It was argued that social work students embarking on a period of practice were learners and needed help to learn. The role of practice *assessor* would not allow for (or capture) this facilitation, possibly leaving it to atrophy. There remains an interesting debate around the core issue of ensuring that whatever assessment models are developed for social work they must correspond to a process of the facilitation of learning. Teaching will take place within the educational programme but it will always have a generic quality as it cannot relate to every possible practice setting in which a student may be placed. Students will always need help in tailoring their learning to fit the setting in which they are placed and developing new learning appropriate to that setting. They cannot therefore just be assessed within that practice setting. Learners need a facilitative environment in which to develop their knowledge, skills and values, make mistakes and learn from them, try out new ideas and ways of working, and have the opportunity to practise their practice. We believe that a facilitative environment needs to be created and that this is a skilled job. The skills of facilitation and enabling can be learnt in the same way as other skills. Once learnt, these skills can then be adapted and applied to other situations where learning is taking place. Many enablers operate across a continuum of learning from pre-qualification awards through professional qualification and onto post-qualification and advanced awards. Not all their skills are used in all areas but the range they have available are generally employed in different packages across the learning continuum.

The post-qualifying framework includes a practice education pathway at the higher specialist (masters) level and advanced awards and a core unit around facilitating the development of others in the specialist (usually level 3) award. It may be that the numbers undertaking post-qualifying training will not meet the need for the increased number of practice learning opportunities required in the social work degree. Practice learning is a central component of all social work education programmes at all levels, but offers far more – being uniquely placed to shape the future of the profession. Enablers in the workplace are the gatekeepers to the profession and the real guides to learning through continuing professional development. In a time of constant change, these wider roles take on even greater significance as social work responds to its changing environment.

Learning in Uncertain and Complex Environments

Social work, as Dominelli warns us, is a 'troubled and troubling profession' (Dominelli, 2004). Troubled by the shifts and eddies of policies affecting the broad arena of social care and the ever increasing managerial emphasis on risk and quality, social work's problems create a profession that seems to lie in doubt. Furthermore, the increase in expectations on the profession, coupled with the lowering of resources, forces the profession to ask hard questions of itself. Professional identity is challenged by the urgency of moves towards multidisciplinary and multi-professional work alongside large-scale Department of Health funded and orientated workforces. Social work struggles to find its place politically. The left may view social workers as 'agents of social control'; the right may view those same people doing the same tasks as 'do-gooders' (Gregory and Holloway, 2005). And, as social work appears to gain acceptance by the state, it becomes less clear who social work serves; the state or the individual? What governs its values and priorities (Stevenson, 2004)?

Sometimes it becomes hard to trace the development of the actual social work task through these changes. One can clearly discern, for example, a diagnostic and therapeutic aspect to the role, based on notions of inclusion, back to the Seebohm Report of 1968, which described a service available to all within a general commitment to increasing and enhancing levels of social citizenship (Gregory and Holloway, 2005). As we know, however, Seebohm led to the unification of social work in generalist departments that formed the basis for subsequent practice – until relatively recently. It has been argued that the generally inhospitable terrain of government agency has broadly been unhelpful and restrictive towards the development of the social work profession, stifling initiative and the creative use of skills (Stevenson, 2005). By the 1990s, and towards the present day, social work is trying to respond to watershed legislation in the key areas of community care (NHS and Community Care Act, 1990) and children and families (Children Act, 1989 and more recently Children Act, 2004), where a different language forms the landscape of understanding for social work: managing outcomes, risk prediction, evidence-based practice and the market economy of care. Indeed, given the supposed ethos of New Labour's broad agenda, some commentators argue that social work faces a tougher time than it did under a conservative administration, and is losing its fundamental emphasis on holistic and caring models in general practice (Jordan, 2001; Cowen, 1999).

Yet, social work, as Dominelli noted, is also *troubling* in its conception of itself. Underpinning all these developments in social work has been the 'post modern condition' – an increasing sense of *uncertainty* in social work (Hugman, 2005). Having broadly developed in scale and ambition over recent decades, the social work profession has had to make certain claims about the efficiency and appropriateness of its interventions – it has had to argue that it 'works'. The questioning of social work's methods and the querying of limitations in the predicative capacity of concepts and techniques has been hard for the profession to deal with. The drive for 'effective' practice when dealing with multiple-problem families and individuals in such complex arenas is severely compromised. Writers from a post-structural theoretical background offer ways forward by critiquing this search for technical certainty, whilst also rethinking the way in which social workers should act in these complex situations (Hugman, 2005). Following this analysis through, Howe (1994) argues that social work is no longer about seeking the 'truth' in any given situation. Such truths, he contends, are fundamentally altered by the meaning different people and groups ascribe to them. Social workers therefore need to work in a way that demonstrates their comprehension of the plurality of meanings that different users bring to the service. These meanings will be different dependent, for example, on how an actor in a given setting perceives themselves in relation to such issues as class, status, age, ethnicity, gender, sexuality and so forth. The same will go for all those involved: significant others and workers in the intervention – learners and enablers too. Social workers therefore must begin to work in a way that demonstrates their understanding of this complexity: involving others in a participative style and, fundamentally, operating in a way that acknowledges their power as the central, perhaps key role in how such interventions are ascribed meaning and given direction (Howe, 1994). Taylor and White (2006) argue that tensions exist in social work education to focus on certainty when the professional context requires 'respectful uncertainty'.

> The more that the uncertainties of practice are acknowledged, the more fervent is the quest for technologies aimed at reducing them. There is a danger that we will become increasingly constrained as educators to focus exclusively on 'education for certainty'. (Taylor and White, 2006, p. 944)

Later chapters in this book go into the detail of some writers in this arena who argue that the issue of critical reflection becomes central to the social workers role in this post-structural world (Fook, 2002; Taylor and White, 2000). Of course, many writers are aware of the descent into meaninglessness if all we see and do as social workers is merely a product of our language and perspective – surely there are some 'truths' about intervention, perhaps based upon our notions of practice wisdom, that cannot so easily be critiqued as products of our power. More specifically, the truths around the experience of service users who suffer disadvantage from structural forces such as unemployment, poor housing and racism cannot be readily dismissed, and surely it is social work's core task to deal with these issues (Smith and White, 1997). Nevertheless, this 'search for certainty' is powerful. Its antecedents in UK political life are shown in the 'what works' debates that characterised policy and practice development in the Probation service through the 1990s – a time during which it lost its connection with the social work profession. Reflecting on this Pinker asserted the importance of practitioner's experience: 'the pressure to base practice on evidence runs the risk of being reduced to an injunction to heed only the results of experimental research, ignoring the wide range of knowledge practitioners bring to bear on their work' (Pinker, 1997, p. 20).

Although to some extent the 'what works' debate has been played out in Probation settings – with the realisation that what works for one might not work for another (Worsley, 2004) – social work has yet to move through this development. Similarly, social work has yet to fully grasp the point made by Pinker, of the importance of the practitioner within the research process. Yet, the growth of such institutions as the Social Care Institute for Excellence (SCIE) tells its own story of the search for certainty. SCIE's role is the dissemination and promotion of knowledge about 'evidence based good practice guidance' in social care (Walter et al., 2004). The search for evidence to direct social work intervention has, of course, its promoters and its critics. The search for certainty can, however, be further evidenced in the pursuit of a whole range of other issues outside of evidence-based practice, such as the development of risk into something of an obsession. Social work is bombarded with 'how to' manuals with uncritical advice about risk assessment and risk management – oblivious to (or in denial about) the complexity of the situation social workers deal with. Indeed, some authors see risk as *the* defining characteristic of social work practice and reduce this kaleidoscope of a profession to 'a process for assessing the likelihood that a given person (usually a parent) will harm a child in the future' (Kemshall and Pritichard, 1996).

Parton, another post-structural writer, also foresaw this new emphasis on risk within social work, placing it within a general growth of increasing managerialist accountability. Within this scenario we see an emphasis on social workers as managers of care services and of 'social risk', with a resultant shift further away from therapeutic interventions (Parton, 1994). For many social workers this particular change has its most obvious expression in the increased amount of monitoring, reporting and general paperwork concerned with the quality agenda, value for money and new professional relationships (Hugman, 2005). Within some of social work's professional relationships – particularly with health services – one can observe clear clashes of culture on a number of levels but particularly, in the context of this analysis, between the medical model's reliance on positivistic forms of knowledge, enquiry and research. It could be argued that in such environments, a greater emphasis is placed on certainty – the *right* answer to the specific health care need. Given all that we have said about social work's growing understanding of complexity and post-structural critique of meaning, social work's new found relationship with health colleagues sees a challenge to the acceptance of complexity and uncertainty with a view that the truth is there to be found by the professional.

ACTIVITY

To begin to think about what social work is and who defines it

Write down a single sentence description of what you think social work 'is'.

Reflect on where your ideas about its definition comes from.

What characteristics of social work might others have that are different from yours? Think of senior managers, service users and central government.

Where does this leave the learner and the enabler? In any shifting pattern of uncertainty, the importance of ongoing learning becomes vital to survival. Schön was aware of this and saw reflective practice as the only way for the professional to survive (Schön, 1983). The development of these ideas through notions of critical (Fook, 2002) and reflexive practice (Taylor and White, 2000) argue an essentially similar point. Practitioners need to create their own awareness and understanding of the situations in which they intervene, through a process of critical and reflective practice. Only in this way, it is argued, can the profession be developed. The over reliance on social work theory and method is mistaken in this analysis, and practitioners need to respond to each situation in a unique way – because no two situations are ever the same. Schön (1983) powerfully described the 'irreducible element of art' within the professional's intervention. For the enabler, it appears that they are left with a new task: *developing the artist*. Learners, as they move through aspects of professional education need to develop far more than just 'doing' skills. The emphasis within the learning partnership must move towards reflection, critical analysis and developing practitioner-based research methodologies. All these aspects of learning and teaching in social work are dealt with in the forthcoming chapters, but the tensions we have ascribed to the learning environment must be considered. We have developed arguments regarding social workers dealing with uncertainty and complexity – but also a concern around a bureaucratised, inflexible, organisational backdrop that might actively mitigate against creative, autonomous, individualised intervention. This is one current challenge for learners and enablers in social work settings: how free are we to learn? The next section looks at the notion of the learning organisation, the other side of this coin, and asks the question, what is the nature of the learning environment?

The Learning Organisation

Given the complexity of the environment in which social workers are making decisions, we can offer some sympathy for learners new to the setting – how are they to understand the intricacies of meaning and power that an experienced practitioner may well have assimilated into their practice many years before? But, beyond the relationship between learner and enabler, how is the organisation going to deal with the complexity of the environment in which it operates? The concept of the learning organisation has its origins within, not surprisingly, the private sector where the need to keep abreast of the unpredictable and dynamic business environment forced business thinkers such as Peter Senge to believe that 'the ability to learn faster than your competitors may be the only sustainable competitive advantage' (Senge, 1990). The notion clearly has many strengths, and it is interesting to reflect on the organisational background of social work and whether it inhabits 'learning organisations' which have been described as:

> Organizations where people continually expand their capacity to create the results they truly desire, where new and expansive patterns of thinking are nurtured, where collective aspiration is set free, and where people are continually learning to learn together. (Senge, 1990, p. 7)

Senge expands our understanding of what it means to be a dynamic, learning organisation – his challenge regarding the 'setting free' of our aspiration is particularly poignant given the ongoing debate about issues such as how free we are to learn and the general level of discretion in social work (see, for example, Evans and Harris, 2004). Senge raises the belief that *all* workers within a learning organisation are learners – that this concept must expand throughout the organisation and certainly beyond the professional roles: it is an individual *and* a collective issue. It is interesting to note that the new GSCC Code of Practice for Employers clearly promotes this notion in its requirement for all social care employers to *provide training and development opportunities to enable social care workers to strengthen and develop their skills and knowledge* (GSCC, 2002, Section 3). How readily we might identify these characteristics within our workplace is obviously a subject for debate and, indeed, one's view of this will perhaps depend upon one's place within the organisation. Nevertheless, we can see from the GSCC's point of view that the new registered workforce should, at least in spirit, exist within a learning organisation. However, it might be useful to pause for a moment and ask ourselves some pertinent questions.

ACTIVITY

To begin to evaluate one's host organisation as a learning organisation

Reflect on the organisation in which you are a learner or enabler. What types of learning does the organisation offer?

- Who provides them?
- How are they accessed?
- How do they link with organisational goals?
- Of what quality are they?
- Are they externally validated?
- How does one benefit by attending? (Registration?)
- Do you have to attend?

Of course, these questions point us towards an analysis of *organisational learning* which looks at how organisations manage their learning, training and skills development. This should be contrasted with the notion of the *learning organisation*, a much broader concept, in line with Senge's ideal definition, that organisational learning works towards. Beyond these training-focused questions we can look to the space the organisation allows for: creative practice, researching practice, the promotion of mentoring relations and team meetings that discuss cases rather than policies. Of course, the stakes within the learning organisation are seemingly quite high. One can argue that an 'unlearning' organisation can be dangerously unresponsive to the changing environment and possess characteristics such as inflexible rules, seeming out of touch, uncooperative managers, poor inter-group interaction, lack of strategic thinking, low levels of consultation and low levels of trust – all often within hierarchical and differentiated structures. The extent to which these factors are present in many statutory or voluntary sector settings is debatable. But what is important is that as learners and enablers in any given setting, we raise our awareness of the nature of the organisation in which we operate. Clearly the situation is not static and the agency within which one works may well be developing ways of working that facilitate notions of learning – indeed, learners and enablers may well be at the forefront of the learning organisation. As Senge notes, 'organizations learn only through individuals who learn. Individual learning does not guarantee organizational learning. But without it no organizational learning occurs' (Senge, 1990, p. 139).

We have earlier considered the complexity and dynamism of the social work environment and, unsurprisingly, this is not a feature of professional life that is, particular to social work. Schön understood this and argued that all of societies institutions are in a state of continuous transformation and that learning within an organisation must be directed at *guiding* such transformations:

> We must, in other words, become adept at learning. We must become able not only to transform our institutions, in response to changing situations and requirements; we must invent and develop institutions which are 'learning systems', that is to say, systems capable of bringing about their own continuing transformation. (Schön, 1973, p. 28)

These ideas are taken forward by a number of writers on the learning organisation and the notion that learning is valuable, and continuous and that every experience is an opportunity to learn comes through forcefully in the literature (Kerka, 1995). Senge, who was the one responsible for popularising the phrase 'learning organisation', understood that for all the rhetoric, learning in organisations that were not conducive or sympathetic to leaning was distinctly problematic. Furthermore, practitioners may lack the tools and guidance they need to make sense of the complexity of the situations they are dealing with. And yet, Senge argues that learning gets to the heart of what it is to be human. As learners and enablers, perhaps we intrinsically know this – being aware of our fulfilment in learning and seeing it as fundamental to our professional lives and our personal growth as people. We regenerate ourselves in these learning environments – within supervision, within sparkling teams and within learning organisations:

> When you ask people about what it is like being part of a great team, what is most striking is the meaningfulness of the experience. People talk about being part of something larger than themselves, of being connected, of being generative. It become quite clear that, for many, their experiences as part of truly great teams stand out as singular periods of life lived to the fullest. Some spend the rest of their lives looking for ways to recapture that spirit. (Senge, 1990, p. 13)

Senge extends this notion beyond the obvious necessity for organisations to learn and adapt in order to survive – he uses the phrase 'generative learning', learning which enhances our capacity to create (Smith, 2001; Senge, 1990). As this is part of what makes us human, it goes that lifelong learning must be an aspect of our professional lives. Of course, this is all very well, but perhaps we, as learners and enablers, do not inhabit organisational cultures that foster this type of learning. Indeed, do we really know of any organisations that have achieved Senge's goals? Is not the bottom line of profit within the private sector really the truth of the learning organisation? Within the plethora of small-scale voluntary sector social care agencies, do any of them really have the infrastructure or inclination to pursue this agenda, given the pressure of short-term funding? And what of the statutory social services departments? Is not their staff development process basically driven by *training* needs as opposed to *development* needs? Finally, bringing this down to the level of learner and enabler – is it not far more easy to teach someone the concrete aspects of professional life – to become our own 'how to' manual? How much harder it can be to teach the intangible, the tacit, the less observable and the less *teachable* (Castells, 2001)? Yet, for all these problems we still have much to thank

Senge for – if nothing else he reminds us of what we should continually aspire to as learners, enablers and strategic thinkers in our organisations and he provides a strong argument for the pursuit of the learning organisation.

So, we finally arrive at the concept of lifelong learning. As students, beginning practitioners and experienced, reflective and research-minded professionals,we continue to learn throughout our career. The central government commitment to this notion is evidenced through a wide range of policies – of which only those to do with social work education will be focussed upon in this volume. However, developments in National Vocational Qualifications (NVQ), Connexions, Careers Guidance, National Training Organisations (e.g. Skills for Care), Individual Learning Accounts and so on are all aspects of the multitude of learning opportunities that are being provided or supported through various initiatives. The European Union also has a comprehensive strategy for lifelong learning which seeks to do the following.

- Guarantee universal and continuing access to learning for gaining and renewing the skills needed for sustained participation in the knowledge society.
- Visibly raise levels of investment in human resources in order to place priority on Europe's most important asset – its people.
- Develop effective teaching and learning methods and contexts for the continuum of lifelong and lifewide leaning. (Gibb, 2002, p. 235)

It is interesting to see here the continuation of themes we have discussed in this chapter – of the need for constant renewal in our skills and knowledge, and the importance of marrying that to appropriate resources within the organisations we inhabit. Our attention is also directed at the need for the way we go about learning and enabling to be appropriate to the settings in which we relate. To be good enablers we must also be continual learners. And, in this sense we retain a knowledge and understanding of what it is to be a learner at the different stages of our professional life. As learners we must also understand our responsibilities to the settings in which we work and the profession to which we seek to belong. As learners we may start out needing to learn the basic pragmatics of our settings, but we must strive to move beyond them into a deeper, broader, more critical understanding of our professional work, our role and the other professionals we may work alongside. Without this depth of critical reflection we do not give our service users our best and surely that must be the central tenet of our professional lives.

Personally, through our own travels as students, practitioners, practice teachers, social work educators and now authors, we understand the difficulties of learning and enabling in settings that do not support and promote the notion of the learning organisation. But we have also had tremendous experiences of working in teams where learning has flourished in a progressive and aspirational manner and working with learners who have refreshed our thinking. We do not pretend that learning and enabling is easy but rather we accept, as the proverb says, that it is better to light one small candle than to curse the darkness.

Key Learning Points

- We learn in a complex and uncertain environment.
- Teaching others needs to be done in a way that acknowledges this complexity.
- The learning organisation and lifelong learning are helpful concepts in the positive development of learners and organisations.
- Learners and enablers need to be critical, reflective and creative practitioners.

CHAPTER 2

Learning Partnerships

The notion of a 'learning partnership' beautifully encapsulates the leap made from pedagogy to andragogy within notions of adult learning: the qualitative differences in how children and adults learn (Knowles, 1980). It appears a stretch to imagine a real sense of partnership between a teacher and a room full of pupils and fortunately that is not our starting point. Our initial task is to construct a partnership between learner and enabler, student and practice teacher, mentor and mentee. We are dealing with how best to enable adults to develop a learning partnership, whilst reflecting on the impact of pedagogical experiences. This chapter aims to explore some key ideas in the construction of a learning partnership which, for all of our talk about partnership, can often be unequal in many regards. Having looked at different aspects of good practice in learning partnerships this chapter will later consider some specific aspects of mentoring, and the chapter as a whole tries to unpick how the notion of partnership can help learners learn. We shall define a learning partnership within social work practice as 'a constructive relationship centred on enabling learning where partners manage the process of utilising learning opportunities for reflection, development and the evaluation and evidencing of professional practice'.

An initial question might be: do we need to have learning partnerships at all? Rogers, for example, underlines how it is vital for the learner to be unconfined:

> Learning is facilitated when the student participates responsibly in the learning process. When he (sic) chooses his own direction, helps to discover his own learning resources, formulates his own problems, decides his own course of action, lives with the consequences of these choices, then significant learning is maximised. (Rogers, 1969, in Gardiner, 1989, p. 56)

But herein lays a problem. Rogers talks of adult learners in the most empowering of scenarios – where the learner is seemingly free to do as he or she chooses, where he or she simply takes responsibility for his or her own choices. Within the sphere of professional education we see that this is a problematic notion. Learners in social care settings can not simply be allowed to make such mistakes because the professional role involves others: the vulnerable, the sick and the disadvantaged within society, not to mention our colleagues within and alongside our professional group. Furthermore, workers within the social care arena operate within legislative, policy and procedural frameworks that circumscribe their actions and indeed, the value base from which they must operate. But, before we discount Rogers as a child of the 1960s, let us ensure we retain his important notion that learning is least effective as an adult when the learner is not given the space to learn; being a learner *has* to mean you are allowed to make mistakes.

Our first thought concerns the situation before the arrival of the learner (or the decision to pursue continuing professional development (CPD) for an existing member of staff) and the preparations that might help create an effective learning partnership; 'to skimp on preparatory work is to set the placement at hazard' (Thompson, Osada and Anderson,1994, p. 25). There are two things that prospective learners and enablers might find useful: an agency/enabler profile and a practice curriculum. Both these activities form a solid base for effective learning partnerships. An agency profile is best understood as a CurriculumVitae for the agency – a snapshot of key aspects of the agency that those new to it can read to capture the essence of the agency (which seems oh! so familiar to its practitioners). It is also an excellent exercise for experienced enablers to try and encapsulate, from their perspective, what they see as the key things someone new to the agency would need to know.

Agency profile – *possible* areas to include are the following:

- Agency – description of the setting, main partners, ethos and mission.
- Team – the team members, multidisciplinary relationships, line management structures.
- Patch – basic demographic information of the geographical area.
- Service user base– key methods of intervention.
- Opportunities for learning, both within the agency and, perhaps, with partners.
- Enabler's profile and approach to supervision.

In constructing such a profile the enabler is empowering the learner, offering them information to illuminate the strange, opaque environment in which they will begin to learn. It sets in place a way of working that promotes openness, clarity and preparedness. Enablers, particularly those with an experienced learner, might consider producing a brief resume of their professional learning – something that demystifies who they are, that captures an understanding of how they got to take on this role whilst avoiding an over enthusiastic trumpeting of achievement.

Practice Curriculum

A practice curriculum can mean many different things to different people but essentially it is a brief outline of the key aspects of learning (policy, procedure and practice) that the new learner will require for a particular setting – a curriculum for practice. As such this concept is less helpful for experienced learners engaged in CPD, but there are elements of the concept that are useful for all. Parker's definition expands the notion somewhat: 'A practice curriculum, in simple terms, is a systematic collection of learning opportunities and experiences designed to meet the demands and needs of a range of stakeholders involved in work based learning' (Parker, 2004, p. 55).

Parker's stakeholders are typically, the learner (student), the The General Social Care Council (GSCC), National Occupational Standards (NOS), the educational institution that is managing the learning and, of course, the enabler (practice teacher). We might also add the host agency, the work-based supervisor (if there is one) and perhaps the host team – all of whom may have a role to play. This is a rather more complex prospect but one which follows on naturally from comments made regarding opportunities in the agency profile. A practice curriculum is exactly as its name suggests – a structured overview of what learning opportunities exist within the placement. It might also contain some notion of the order these would be introduced and how long they may go on for. There might also be reference to different specialist areas of knowledge within the broad team's members and in what styles the learning might be provided – casework, observation, discussion, reading, co-working and so forth. Finally, there might also be some comments that allow the learner to see how the learning opportunities offered might link to the criteria of assessment (e.g. NOS). An example might include as listed in the following table:

Area of learning	Link to standards / key roles	Link to team	Suggested period of engagement
Induction: key policies (list), and procedures (list)	Key role 5 (Manage and be accountable for own practice)	PT, team leader, work-based supervisor	First two weeks
Small caseload of young offenders subject to court orders	All Key roles	Managed by practice teacher, joint working with various team members	Building up caseload towards mid-placement, then review
Court reports/ court duty	Key role 2 Social work practice Key role 3 Support others Key role 5	J. Bloggs, court duty officer for court duty. Practice teacher allocates reports in liaison with team leader	First month – three court visits. Allocation of first court report at two months, then ongoing fortnightly allocation. Review at mid point
Group work – cognitive behavioural approach	All Key roles	J. Jones runs the group – will provide feedback. Mostly observation with opportunities to lead two later sessions	After mid-placement
Supervision	Key role 1–5 Key role 6 Demonstrate competence	Practice teacher	Weekly, ongoing through the placement

By delivering such things as an agency profile and producing a suggested practice curriculum (it would normally be appropriate to discuss with the learner what they were interested in learning about) – the enabler begins in an effective, empowering manner that models inclusivity.

But what of the learner? We need to understand that the significant demands of the academic curriculum will have made an impact for beginning learners, as will workloads for the experienced. One might reasonably expect the learner to provide an overview of their learning – some social work qualifying programmes provide this in their programme handbooks. It might also be that the beginning learner will have taken some time to consider some literature relevant to the placement setting. Indeed, the enabler may have indicated some useful texts in the informal meeting. 'The success of a placement will be enhanced by the amount of prior preparation by the practice teacher, the tutor and the student' (Ford and Jones, 1987, p. 15).

ACTIVITY

Construct profiles of your agency and/or yourself to enhance the inception of a learning partnership

Construct a profile of yourself as a practitioner and an enabler. What boundaries and concerns do you encounter in compiling this – and how might a learner similarly be concerned?

Construct a profile of yourself as a learner identifying your recent learning, your experience, your professional areas of interest and reflections on how you learn best.

Construct your own agency profile and ask a colleague to look over it. Do you see the team setting in the same way?

The Initial Meeting

It is common practice for enablers to meet with learners prior to the learning partnership being formally agreed. The word *informal* meeting is sometimes used for social work students first meeting with their practice teacher but the reality is often that the meeting is anything but informal. Remarkably little research has been conducted into these meetings, although they can often assume a surprising level of importance. It is essential for both parties to avoid inappropriate and premature prejudicial views. Parker makes an excellent point in noting that beginning learners, 'should be proactive in seeking a meeting as this will help (the student) develop skills as a learner with some responsibility for creating and developing experiences in practice' (Parker, 2004, p. 53).

There are essentially only two questions to focus upon: Will there be a sufficient range of opportunities to provide the learner with evidence against the range of standards? How will the learning partnership 'work'? For the learner, it can often be that they have little or no choice with regard to placement or enabler and this can lead to the stretching of flexibility a little too far. Enabler's would do well to retain an awareness of this and, when appropriate, move into an honest appraisal of the partnership's viability. It is in no one's interest for the process to fail for avoidable reasons. Learners and enablers may also wish to reflect on issues such as their attitude and approach to punctuality, time management skills, confidentiality and personal appearance. Another relevant topic, particular to social work students, is that of 'fitness for practice' and preparation for placement. The Department of Health (DH) Requirements of Social Work Training states in section 'K' that programmes must: 'ensure that all students undergo assessed preparation for direct practice to ensure their safety to undertake practice learning in a service delivery setting' (DoH, 2002, p. 4).

The GSCC underlines this and also requires programmes to ensure that students are *fit for practice* – this often takes the form of satisfactory Criminal Records Bureau (CRB) and Health checks but can include some 'signing off' of the student as ready to go out on placement, committed to the values of social work and, 'have the potential to develop high quality professional knowledge and skills that are essential to practice as a social worker' (GSCC, 2002, p. 21).

Qualifying learners should be coming to the placement setting equipped, in general terms, to engage with the learning opportunities. Learners are just that – learners – and should not be expected to arrive as the finished article. Enablers should avoid interrogating learners as to their knowledge about a particular area of practice, and should not appear to be selecting learners by interview. Some social work settings argue that their specialist nature means that they are only suitable for final year learners. However, we feel the emphasis should be on the nature of the learning opportunities. Any setting should be able to offer any learner suitable learning opportunities without confusing the role of learner with colleague. The daunting nature of arriving for an 'informal' meeting must also be acknowledged by the enabler and consideration given to when and where the meeting should take place. It might be helpful to imagine that learners and enablers are bringing equal opportunities to the table at this meeting which can focus on capitalising on the best that both have to offer.

Creating a Learning Agreement

Many learners and enablers confuse the idea of a learning agreement with the pre-placement agreement (PPA) when they are aimed at two separate, albeit similar issues. A learning agreement (or supervision contract) is the drawing up of an agreement about the nature and function of supervision during the learning experience being provided – such agreements should arguably be a feature of *all* learning partnerships. Conversely, PPAs are agreements between practice teacher, student and tutor/social work programme which establish the overarching nature of the placement in terms of workload, supervision, agency policy and so forth. PPAs are a common aspect of qualifying training and form a contractual bridge between the agency and social work programme. We will discuss a range of issues that might arise in both these agreements.

Length, frequency and duration of supervision

For learners and enablers in post-qualifying (PQ) structures who are both likely to be managing learning in conjunction with heavy caseloads and beginning learners whose experience of supervision may be limited, it is vital to contract around when meetings should take place, where and for how long. It might also be helpful to discuss what might and might not be considered appropriate reasons for rearranging. For student learners, Central Council for Education and Training in Social Work (CCETSW) – the predecessor of the GSCC used to promote the notion of supervision within the DipSW structures as lasting for about one and a half hours per (full time) week. There are many permutations on this but it might be useful to outline the parameters around a norm of a minimum of one hour per five working days. This can often be altered to two hours per fortnight (especially where there is an off-site enabler). The key variables to consider include the level of informal supervision, the presence of work based supervisors and the ability of the learner. The social work qualifying degree carries no indication of how often supervision should take place, but individual programmes may have guidance. Of course, PQ mentor/ees would not meet so regularly and likewise may have guidance on levels of supervision. The important point is achieving clarity about how often supervision occurs.

Note-taking and agenda setting

Practice on supervision notes varies enormously amongst programmes, learners and enablers. All agree that there is a need to take supervision notes, but there is occasionally disagreement on who should take the notes. On the one hand, some argue that where the enabler has a formal role of assessor in the process, it is inappropriate to delegate note-taking to the (less powerful) learner who might, theoretically, have to ensure that agenda items containing their poor practice were written in language satisfactory to the enabler – an uncomfortable if not impossible task. Others argue that such problems would be unusual and it can be a developmental process for the learner to have experience of note-taking at these formal sessions on an alternate basis, allowing the enabler to model his or her good practice. Again it is clarity which is the requisite item here – but a compromise might be for the enabler to begin, with the learner, if appropriate to take notes later in the relationship. With regard to agenda setting it is often seen that this is a shared activity and supervision contracts can specify when such agendas are set (the day before or in the first five minutes of the session etc.) and that both parties have a duty to bring items to supervision. Agenda setting is important to focus on for its simple effectiveness in broadening out supervision from the dangers of overly focusing on case management. Many enablers produce pro formas with semi-fixed agendas covering items such as: cases for discussion, feedback, evidence for portfolio, anti-oppressive practice, theory into practice, agreed tasks and agenda setting for next meeting.

Specific learning needs

Many enablers have anxieties about working with, for example, dyslexic learners and in turn those learners can be very apprehensive (often with good reason) about discussing their difficulties. It is important to clarify who will provide what, and in what way, for these particular needs. The programme or agency should have made an assessment of the student's learning needs, and enablers should be made aware of any learning plan that may have resulted and of any aids (such as a laptop) that have been provided. The agency, in turn, should look at how it will handle these needs as it would for any other employee. The stakeholders should discuss at an initial meeting how these needs can be best met. The Disability Discrimination Act (1995) introduced the requirement of 'reasonable adjustments' in the workplace for issues of disability. This can be challenging for many organisations and the lack of a definition of what is 'reasonable' can be frustrating. Learners are all too aware of the potential for discrimination in the workplace (and many do not disclose for that very reason) and enablers must strive to deal with these issues positively, reflecting (and planning) with the learner on how learning opportunities might best be provided given the learning needs. For example, one learner with dyslexia has said: 'People perceive it as you being unable to keep up with the rest of the team. Or not being able to write as well as the team, that you were a hindrance to the group. That they would have to pull you through' (quoted in Wray et al. 2005, p. 9).

This quote is one of a number in a good practice guide publication by the Professional Education and Disability Support Project at the University of Hull. This excellent guide outlines good practice for beginning learners, enablers and social work programmes (see www.hull.ac.uk/pedds). The problems of disentangling the issues of disability, competence and suitability are considered, as is the sadly common experience of learners with disabilities feeling that they receive less than first-class treatment:

> Yes, I feel that my placement choices have been very limited as a direct result of my disability. I believe that many social service departments did not want me because they would have to 'find room' for my support team and my hearing dog and were not prepared to put up with the inconvenience. (quoted in Wray et al. 2005, p. 40)

Competency frameworks

The social work degree is fully tied into the NOS (TOPSS, 2002). Slightly different systems exist in England, Wales, Scotland and Northern Ireland. For experienced learners engaged in CPD they will most likely be producing evidence against PQ competency frameworks such as the specialist award for children and young people, their families and carers (GSCC, 2005). In terms of a learning agreement, both parties need to be clear which standards need to be evidenced and in what way. The most common problem with competency frameworks is that they are not studied sufficiently. Learners and enablers alike can be put off by their length and detail. Alas, there is no shortcut and early contact in the learning partnerships must ensure that all parties understand how the connection between the learning opportunities and the competencies or standards is to be made.

Other elements which might be included in a learning agreement include:

* Confidentiality.
* Support – dealt with below.
* Anti-oppressive practice (developing awareness of issues in practice *and* in the supervisory relationship).
* Venue.
* Timekeeping.
* Review (how effective is this supervisory relationship?).

ACTIVITY

To begin to think about the connection between learning agreements and the ongoing learning partnership

Ellie Fisher is a beginning learner on her first practice placement. It is her third supervision session, and she has completed 30 days out of the 100. Her enabler, Mary, has become concerned that Ellie is very quiet in the team and that colleagues have begun to express some concerns about her effectiveness in her work with people, as she has now moved on past induction, has stopped 'shadowing' other workers, and is starting to work with her own workload. Ellie's enabler decides, as the session progresses, to make a note of Ellie's responses to ideas or suggestions. Here is a selection of Ellie's responses:

* 'They wouldn't let me do that.'
* 'That's not really me.'
* 'I always put things that way.'
* 'I have to finish at 5.'
* 'If only there was more time to work on that.'
* 'I've met him 3 times now, and each time he's made me angry.'
* 'That's just my way of working.'
* 'I have to do that.'
* 'It's just a non-starter.'

After the session, Mary thinks about Ellie's responses, and is able to come to certain conclusions, and to decide what to say at the next session, which she decides to bring forward to the following week.

What do you think Ellie's learning needs are?

How might a practice curriculum be reviewed prior to Mid Placement Review in the light of this?

What aspects of a learning agreement might be useful to return to?

Complete the following grid.

Activity/learning	How is this to be achieved	How will this be measured	Timescale

Source: adapted from Beale (2005); Littler (2005).

Support for the Learner and the Enabler

Hawkins and Shohet (2000) are in a surprisingly small group of writers who pay attention to the support needs of the enabler as well as the learner in the learning partnership. Whilst Kadushin's (1976) construction of supervision outlines educative, supportive and administrative functions, the clear message is that the support of the learner is the prime concern. In the many models of supervision that are offered in this field, the notion of support can often be implicit rather than explicit, especially for the enabler (Parker, 2004). Nevertheless, particularly for beginning learners, the need for support is self-evident. The learner can be a stranger in a strange land, surrounded by uncertainty, unconnected to colleagues and isolated from his or her student peers. Hence, many learning contracts explicitly include a section on support. The learning partnership needs to reflect carefully on this issue and enablers would do well to contemplate their agency's structures for support and how accessible they are for learners as well as themselves. Providers of social work education often deliver 'in-college' days which possess a supportive element, some deliver ongoing learning groups throughout with a similar purpose. Learners and enablers should be encouraged to also think beyond these givens into their wider support network – support isn't confined to the profession.

ACTIVITY

To raise learners' and enablers' awareness of the available networks that can support different aspects of the learning partnership

Take a large sheet of (flip chart) paper and draw, at the centre, a symbol or picture of yourself and then around that draw pictures, symbols, diagrams or words to represent all the things and people that support you in learning and being creative at work.

What is the nature of the connection between you and the source of support? Using a different colour, draw on the paper things that block you from using your support.

Looking at the overall picture – do you have the kind of support you want? Is it enough? Is something missing? Perhaps you need to develop an action plan to improve your support system.

Source: Hawkins and Shohet (2000, p. 18).

As a learner, one is often able to access a range of support opportunities – this may not necessarily be the case for the enabler. There is no doubt that creating a learning partnership carries stress for the enabler, perhaps combining this task with an already full workload, and the enablers need to ensure that he or she are able to model good practice by considering their own support needs, as well as their learners. What support opportunities does the agency provide for enablers? Are these appropriate, accessible and helpful? Perhaps such structures do not already exist and the enabler may wish to reflect, as we noted above in the exercise – what alternative strategies can be developed for the provision of support. All these questions form a broader debate – how importantly do we take our support needs? Often, when doing time management exercises with learners one can discover how fragile their commitment to their own support needs can be. When confronted with choices amongst professional tasks, supportive engagements can be the first to go. Enablers may model poor practice in similar behaviour. The challenges of professional practice are such that ongoing attention to support needs is a necessity, not a pleasant option.

Mentor and Mentee Learning Partnerships

While the general approach of this book is to illustrate the similarities in learning and enabling relationships across social work, there are obvious differences in equality between experienced and beginning learners in partnership with enablers. The skilled practitioner learner looks for a different type of learning partnership with an enabler. Practitioner learners (often PQ candidates) are typically working with an enabler who may be a PQ mentor (perhaps external to the agency), colleague, team leader or staff development officer. These variations can all affect the nature of the learning relationship but, in essence, we are considering a mentor and a mentee partnership. Here are two helpful definitions of mentoring which aim to capture the particular flavour of this learning partnership: 'To help and support people to manage their own learning in order to maximise their potential, develop their skills, improve their performance and become the person they want to be' (Parsloe). 'Off-line help from one person to another in making transitions in knowledge, work or thinking' (Megginson and Clutterbuck) (from Clutterbuck, 2004, p. 12).

The characteristics that are emanating from these definitions point us towards an enabling, developmental relationship to do with reflection and skill development. The notion of *transition* is particularly attractive as it encourages images of movement and change within the learner, whilst the phrase 'off-line' is used not to discern some amorphous supervision by software – but rather a relationship outside of the line of management. The whole speaks to the greater concept of equity in the learning partnership of mentor and mentee – they are equals, most commonly in the sense of being qualified social workers. But, does this take us much distance from partnerships around qualifying placements? Exploring this concept of mentor in more detail we typically encounter the following shared notions:

- learning partnerships built on trust;
- provision of support and development opportunities;
- reflection on issues and blockages presented by the mentee;
- professional growth.

Clutterbuck's approach helps encapsulate the differing aspects and axes of mentoring and facilitates comparison accords different types of learning partnership. For enablers who are mentors one can delineate these core elements: *Coaching* – which can be viewed as a relatively directive means of helping someone develop competence. *Counselling* (not in a therapeutic sense) relates to the action of being a 'sounding board', listening and supporting. *Networking* can refer to information networks as well as people-centred networks – helping mentees find out what they need to know and developing self-resourcefulness. *Guiding*, or providing guidance, almost being a guardian – can often relate primarily to advice giving. Thus, these four elements form aspects of the mentor/mentee learning partnership – with the elements in relatively differing proportions according to the nature and expectations of the learning partnership. Let's portray them as shown in Diagram 2.1.

We could broadly argue that beginning learning partnerships tend to draw mostly from the top half of this diagram with more of an emphasis on directive qualities around coaching and guiding. Experienced learners as mentees with mentors perhaps enjoy a less directive learning environment that whilst involving stretching and nurturing, will more readily follow counselling and networking agendas. How can we apply some of the thinking in this analysis? Pegg (1999) takes this notion into a more pragmatic arena by describing his Five C Model of

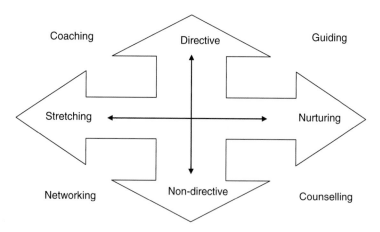

Diagram 2.1 Four elements of the mentor/mentee learning partnership

running a mentoring session, noting that there are differences between 'pushing' and 'pulling' within the relationship – areas where mentors will be more directive, and others where mentors will be trying to stretch the mentee. It will be useful to take Pegg's model and apply it to learners and enablers in a social work setting – as we try to unpack the nature of the learning partnership as it applies to mentors and mentees:

Challenges: What are the goals for the session? What issues need to be discussed? What are the challenges that present themselves in the workplace? What are the requirements of the learning partnership – what is required to complete the portfolio of learning, for example? What are the mentee's strengths, what are the areas for development? In unpacking these challenges, what workload relief for the learning process might be considered?

Choices: This leads into a discussion of what choices should be made to meet the challenges that lie ahead – it might be a discussion of workload management techniques. It might be the discussion of different ways of achieving the same ends. Thus, for example, having identified material required for a portfolio, the mentor and mentee may enter discussions on which order these should be prepared in, which items will meet which competencies best and what direct evidence may best support reflective accounts. Finally, challenges may exist around the mentee's learning – perhaps they find it difficult to 'reflect'. The mentor may facilitate discussion on how best to develop skills in this area by the use of exercises, discussion and observation.

Consequences: This, rather more straightforwardly, is the exploration of the outcomes of choices – what are the pros and cons of pursuing the choices you are interested in making? Some people prefer to rate such things numerically. Pegg (1999) suggests that mentors and mentees check out their gut feelings on some of these consequences.

Creative Solutions: Pegg reminds us that creative, imaginative practice is often effective, so what would be a different view of the choices one is thinking of making – what if things were approached back to front? Sometimes, for example, our closeness to work (and its pressures) makes it hard to take more objective, 'outside' view akin to those of a hired consultant. There may also be others in the team that have been through this process, whose advice could be invaluable.

Conclusions: Bringing the thoughts, actions and reflections together to construct a measured, realistic and achievable constructive way forward. Perhaps, if the mentee is working towards the achievement of something difficult, unsure of whether the learning partnership can achieve its aim, it might be worthwhile having a 'back-up' plan.

Pegg's helpful Five C model is quite typical of the literature in this area, most of which is often directed at private sector scenarios. This brief taste of some of the literature in the mentoring field has hopefully made the point that learning partnerships with beginning and experienced learners share many things in common. However, those involved in mentoring relationships within PQ structures may wish to delve further into some of the broader literature. There is remarkably little written on mentoring within the social work context. Team leaders in social work settings often blur the boundaries between different forms of supervision, perhaps *having* to ensure that they focus on practical workload management issues but *wanting* to develop a supervisory style closer to a mentoring relationship. One might further reflect that this stems from the powerful experience of learning at the point of entry into the profession – with the practice teacher. However, there are evident dangers in assuming that a mentoring style can work within hierarchical work relationships – how free is the mentee to discuss his or her errors? How free are they to discuss their views of the organisation? How free are they to discuss issues of difference?

Working with Difference

Working with difference in a learning partnership is an ongoing aspect of the process of learning just as much as reflection, skill development and the increase of knowledge. This is partly because everyone we work with as learners or enablers – be they clients or colleagues will possess some qualities and characteristics that are different from ourselves. That said, if we turn the lens around on ourselves as a professional group, we might consider how our professional group reflects the communities it serves. About 80 per cent of social workers are white and similarly 80 per cent are female. Of course, the picture varies enormously within the figure with areas such as Derbyshire having 99 per cent white social workers, to Inner London where 48 per cent are from black and ethnic minority groups (DoH, 2005). The point raised is that as within our professional group, the learning partnerships we inhabit are likely to reflect similar elements of diversity. It will be quite usual for many learning partnerships to be white and female. It will be relatively unusual, especially in certain areas, for someone who is black or male to be involved in the learning partnership. As enablers, one has to take this into account when constructing a notion of power within the learning partnership. Clearly, we should be familiar with the potential for disadvantage when confronting issues of discrimination – and these differences have a similar potential to disadvantage learners in social work settings as they do receivers of services. As a professional group we should all be committed to notions of anti-discriminatory practice (ADP) and anti-oppressive practice – whereby we seek to combat oppression and discrimination in the way we go about our professional lives. 'Anti-discriminatory practice is an attempt to eradicate discrimination and oppression from our own practice and challenge them in the practice of others and in the institutional structures in which we operate' (Thompson, 1997, p. 33).

This must apply equally to our work with service users as to ourselves as learners or enablers. Of course, as enablers we might wish to assist learners in the development of their understanding of oppression as it applies to practice. However, we must also consider the issue as it relates to the learning partnership. This is not always straightforward and not always simply about power. Sinclair, for example, considers how, with regard to supervision, black students queried not having the choice of a black supervisor, expressing the view that this would have helped them to open up more easily about their work. They felt that a black tutor or supervisor 'acted as a visible role model with whom the student could identify' (Sinclair, 1990, p. 6). The scenarios we are facing can be complex, indeed some argue that supervision has a 'more complex ethical sensitivity' than work with service users (Hawkins and Shohet, 2000, p. 48). As social workers we are familiar with the structural nature of power and its scenarios of oppression linked to race, gender, sexuality, religion and disability – but if we approach difference in a critical light we can see the potential dangers inherent in settings where, for example, the learner is the only male. Thus, what we construct as a relatively powerful structural difference when we observe society need not necessarily apply (or apply to the same extent) in settings where other forms of power might be apparent – experience, qualifications, membership of a team and so on.

By way of illustration of this complexity let us briefly explore two small case studies using structural matters that perhaps get less attention than others. The first scenario is where the learner is older than the enabler and has a wealth of experience as an unqualified worker in the same setting. In this case we see that despite differences in the status of enabler and qualification held, it is not difficult to imagine a balance of power leaning towards the learner side of the partnership. Second, we can envisage a scenario where the learner may have a relatively affluent class background, perhaps an MA student who has graduated from a prestigious university – again one can envisage a shift in the balance of power, where the enabler might feel restricted in offering (constructive) critical feedback about agency writing styles, communication and 'connection' with service users. Class, as a structural phenomenon has appeared to slip off social work's radar in recent years and yet, whether within service user's lives or learning partnerships, can still be a powerful force. How do learners and enablers deal with these complex power relationships within the learning partnership? The first step of any journey is often the hardest and *awareness* is the initial premise. Both parties need to reflect on this issue and to share in the construction of mutual understanding of roles and responsibilities. It will be interesting to take Thomson, Osada and Anderson's (1994) erudite and illuminating description of learning strategies around ADP, which focused on practice learning, and apply it to the learning partnership. Of course, these ideas also construct some guidance on strategies around broader ADP learning.

Thomson, Osada and Anderson's first strategy focuses on the 'hypothetical approach': *What if this learner / enabler were …?* This form of questioning can be useful in stimulating ideas on how we respond to different cultural backgrounds and needs. Enablers can reflect on the composition of staffing in their agency and the general provisions of services. The second strategy is called 'de-individualisation'. Breaking free of the bonds of individual casework will always be hard for social workers whose environments often focus inherently on the individual. Enablers should retain an awareness of the broader picture that exists when working with learners, for example, different cultural backgrounds – reflecting on the social contexts in which they live and particularly their membership of oppressed groups. A learner with a disability may benefit from reflection on the organisational and professional examples of those who have managed learning in these environments. The third strategy is to 'block destructive processes' and Thomson, Osada and Anderson outline four such processes that can be harmful to developing good awareness: tokenism, dogmatism, hierarchy of oppression and minimisation. 'Tokenism' can be described as simply going through the motions without actually engaging properly with the core values of ADP. Within the learning partnership we must ensure that differences are understood and dealt with sensitively, where 'questioning before challenging' as an approach indicates the importance we place on moving learners and enablers on, rather than making them defensive. 'Dogmatism' can be seen as the reduction of complex networks of meaning to simple, crude and rigid answers. With issues of ADP there is no one answer, rather we must strive to understand the complex needs of the learning partnership and not make assumptions that, for example, learners with dyslexia should be supported in particular ways. Neither learners nor enablers should be dogmatic; one approach to issues of power or difference should not be thought of as *the* answer (even if it is someone's pet theory), rather a constructively critical approach should be fostered. 'Hierarchy of oppression' refers to the notion that we can construct pyramids of disadvantage with the most important at the top, and the least important at the bottom. Arguments around whether race is a more significant factor in oppression rather than gender are ultimately unsatisfactory. Learners (or enablers) may have a particular interest in one area of disadvantage, such as disability, but the learning partnership should not allow this to dominate at the expense of other aspects of disadvantage where the learner may not be demonstrating appropriate levels of awareness. Thompson, Osada and Anderson (1994) make the useful suggestion of focusing on commonalties in learning – such as power, stereotypes and the transfer of learning from understanding one aspect of disadvantage to another. The final destructive process is 'minimisation'. This occurs when oppression gets played down. Learners and particularly enablers must be sensitive to this tendency and not play down, for example, the impact of differences in the gender, race, age and so forth of the learner and enabler.

Another strategy for learning partnerships is 'perspective transformation'. This is a term coined by Mezirow who considers how we become aware of the learned assumptions we have that shape the way we see ourselves and our relationships. Perspective transformation is, 'reconstituting this structure to permit a more inclusive and discriminating integration of experience and acting upon these new understandings' (Mezirow, 1981, pp. 6–7). For learners and enablers, this is about awareness of assumptions within the learning partnership, ongoing processes of reflection and critical evaluation of ourselves as learners and enablers – not just ourselves as practitioners. The learning partnership should ensure that time is spent in reviewing itself in the light of ADP. Finally, 'sensitivity to language' is as important within the learning partnership as it is to our constructs of service users. We are all aware of how language can both create and reinforce divisions in society – excluding (chair*man*), dehumanising (*the disabled*), infantilisation (*the office girls*) and stigmatisation (*black mark*). So, of course, we must be wary of applying these language problems within the learning partnerships we inhabit – avoiding phrases such as *the student*, whilst not creating an air of defensiveness that hinders self-expression (adapted from Thompson, Osada and Anderson, 1984, pp. 17–23).

ACTIVITY

Using the GSCC Code of Practice to explore some of Thomson, Osada and Anderson's strategies for learning about ADP

Learners and enablers should familiarise themselves with the GSCC Code of Practice for social care workers, particularly Sections 1 and 2

1. Take a closer look at Section 2 of the Code – explore in supervision how its contents might be applied to the learning partnership. What translates easily and what would be harder to transfer?
2. Now consider Section 1 of the Code more closely and substitute the word 'learner' for 'service user'. How does the learning partnership deal with the issues such a revised code might raise?
3. Finally, reflect on the language of the Code, its authors, its purpose and its political context.

Learning partnerships, as we have seen, are complex relationships. Enablers have a difficult job in getting the right balance between their different, perhaps competing aspects. We have outlined the importance of good beginnings with the use of profiles and practice curricula and focused particularly on the foundation stone of the learning agreement. We would argue that if the learning partnership can arrive at a constructive and mutual agreement about how learning will take place then it becomes far more likely that positive learning and relationships will accrue. However, just because one sets sail on a calm sea does not mean there will be no storms ahead. Learning partnerships must pay attention to support needs and particularly the impact of difference. ADP should not be seen as a subject for discussion linked solely to intervention and agency practice. It should be actively and overtly discussed as it applies to the learning partnership. Differences (and similarities) within such relationships can have a profound impact on their functioning and their modelling of professional practice. They can either form a misty or clear lens through which professional practice can be examined. It is better to have as unobstructed a view of the world as we can.

Key Learning Points

- Learning partnerships need planning.
- Agency profiles and learning curricula are positive foundations. Learners need to prepare as well as enablers.
- Learning contracts help clarify roles, responsibilities and the shape of learning partnerships. Off-site enablers must ensure that contracts are appropriate to the partnership arrangements.
- Mentors and mentee relationships have qualitatively different learning partnerships.
- Difference within all learning partnerships should be acknowledged.

CHAPTER 3

Adult Learning

This chapter will introduce the reader to the various factors influencing learning. Key messages from the different schools of thought will be highlighted to help the reader link the theory with his or her practice. Activities are included to help the readers identify factors which may influence the way that they learn. These activities can then be used with any learner with whom they are working to consider differences and similarities which may influence their learning relationship.

The two phrases 'lifelong learning' and 'you can't teach an old dog new tricks' are both in common usage and clearly contradictory. The key to this discrepancy may be found in the words 'learning' and 'teach'. Our society is changing so fast that we need people to be life-long learners, continually learning new knowledge and skills so that the workforce can adapt to current needs. Yet, for many the experience of being taught as a child was so negative that they find the idea of continuing to be taught unattractive. Learning and teaching are not necessarily synonymous. We are all familiar with the adult who has knowledge or skills, which they were never taught and we were all probably taught to do things which we never actually learnt. 'The simple difference is that teaching requires two participants, a learner and a teacher, whereas learning requires only one, a learner. Furthermore even when a teacher is teaching it does not guarantee that learning takes place' (Evans, 1999, p. 31).

This chapter will be about facilitating people to learn. We have deliberately chosen the term 'enabler' to refer to the person who is involved with facilitating the learning process rather than the term 'teacher'. This is because we see the 'enabling role' as wider than the role of teacher. The process of enabling an adult to learn is different from that of teaching a child. Adults come to learning more as equals, with previous experiences and knowledge, which can be used as building blocks for future development.

41

Knowles (1980, 1984 and 1989) coined and developed the concept of 'andragogy' to explain how adults learn. He contrasts this with 'pedagogy' which is about teaching children. Knowles argues that pedagogy was the only educational model until the middle of the twentieth century, used with adults and children alike. In pedagogy the teachers have full responsibility for the learning process. They decide what will be learned, how and when it will be learned, and if it has been learned. The role of the learner is passive and dependent, entailing following the teacher's instructions. Knowles argues that as individuals mature, their needs change. They become more self-directing, they need to organise their learning around the problems they meet in their lives, they need to determine what they need to know and when they need to learn it. So the pedagogical approach does not meet their needs. Thus a different approach is needed. This he refers to as 'andragogy'. Certain key ideas about how adults learn are embodied in the model, which have implications for the enabling role. These are as follows:

- Adults need to know why they need to learn something. They have their own motivations for learning: the purposes for learning are related to their real lives, and the roles they undertake.
- Adults have a readiness to learn when they need that learning to cope effectively with life. Timing of the learning is therefore important and will be most effective when it coincides with a need to learn. The enabler's function is therefore to identify current learning needs with the learner.
- Adults generally prefer to be self-directing. They initiate the learning and the enabler's function is to provide an environment in which this learning can take place.
- Adults come to learning with a variety of experiences. The richest source for learning often lies within these experiences. Hence the role of the enabler may be to use techniques, which tap into these experiences.
- Adult orientation to learning is problem- or a task-centred rather than subject-centred. Adults need to apply knowledge to specific problems rather than learn ideas, and so on in the abstract. Obviously for some adults the pursuit of knowledge for its own sake is satisfying but generally adults seek knowledge to help them solve problems.

Knowles originally presented his model of 'andragogy' as the antitheses to pedagogy. He later revised this idea and suggested that the models could be complimentary. The models are based on different assumptions, for example, pedagogy has the assumption that learners are motivated by grades whereas adults are more self-motivated. Knowles argues that the role of the enabler is therefore to check which assumptions are realistic in any given situation. Adult learners are often dependent; for example, when they are entering a totally new area of knowledge or when they have no experience in a particular area. Thus, they may need the enabler to identify what they need to learn. The greatest difference would then be how the enabler continued his or her task. The 'androgog' would then encourage the learner to take increasing responsibility for his or her own learning. Possibly by providing a climate in which learners feel safe to learn, explaining to them how the new learning would assist them in their work, giving them some responsibility for choosing methods and resources for their learning and involving them in the evaluation of their learning.

Many writers argue that Knowles' assumptions underlying andragogy are neither based on research findings nor is it a psychological analysis of the learning process (Jarvis, 1996; Tennant, 1997). Yet it is a popular notion in the field of adult education and links with the ideas of the Humanist School of psychology.

ACTIVITY

To assist you in considering general factors which may have influenced your own learning and may then be generalised to the learning of others:

Think of something which you consider you have learnt to do well.

What factors helped you to learn?

Think of something which you have 'failed' to learn.

What factors inhibited your learning?

Race (2000) has undertaken this exercise numerous times and from the results concluded that the four key factors for successful learning are as follows:

- Motivation – having some reason to undertake the learning, either intrinsic motivation, such as the desire for self development or extrinsic motivation, such as the acquisition of a qualification or promotion.

- Feelings – having positive feedback about the learning process.
- Doing – having the chance to practice, make mistakes and learn from the mistakes.
- Understanding – being given information in accessible forms, having time to digest and assimilate new knowledge and skills with existing knowledge and skills.

Learners in the workplace need all these factors in place if they are to succeed.

Theories of Learning

Theories about learning are generally found within the wider discipline of psychology. They basically split into two camps: those which see learning as concerned with processes going on within any individual and those which see learning as influenced by social context and interaction. These camps can be further subdivided. None of the major schools of learning theorists give full explanations for all aspects of learning but each have pointers for enablers to use in their practice with a learner.

The Behavioural School

This school bases its view of human behaviour primarily on observable behaviours rather than attitudes, knowledge and beliefs. Much of the work came from studies on animals and as such may not always be directly applicable to humans. The behaviourists, for example, Pavlov, Watson and Skinner (Tennant, 1997) argue that behaviour, which is reinforced in some way, will be repeated. Complex tasks can be broken down into small steps which then are built up again by reinforcement. These theories tend to be centred on the activities of the enabler rather than the learner. This school deals primarily with behaviour: it does nothing to address our understanding of how concepts and knowledge are acquired. The definition of learning in this school is a change in behaviour. Reinforcement is defined as anything which will ensure that behaviour is repeated; usually something which is pleasurable to the learner. Sometimes the word used is reward but this is not strictly the case as reinforcement can be the removal of something unpleasant like anxiety.

Petty (2005) uses the Behaviourist model to explain motivation and demotivation. He suggests that labelling and reinforcing a learner's success (e.g. by praise) encourages the learner to develop, to take risks and increases motivation. It is also a basis for later constructive criticism by building security and confidence. He calls this cycle the 'Virtuous Cycle' (see Diagram 3.1).

He compares this with the 'Vicious Cycle' where the learner is demotivated through criticism and fear of failure. This is akin to the experience of many returning adults who claim poor previous learning experiences. Petty argues that reinforcement is the most effective way of improving learner performance (see Diagram 3.2).

The enabler could utilise some of the ideas from the Behavioural School by considering how complex tasks may be broken down into manageable steps. When a learners successfully complete a step they should be given something they consider pleasurable to reinforce the learning. This may be praise or something tangible such as a nice coffee. Subsequent steps are treated in the same way until the task is complete. Reinforcement should be fairly immediate, so regular feedback is important in establishing behaviours. When learners are not motivated, special forms of reinforcement may be necessary. In our experience even when working with adults chocolate bars, certificates and medals work well.

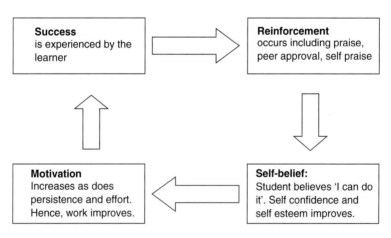

Diagram 3.1   Virtuous cycle

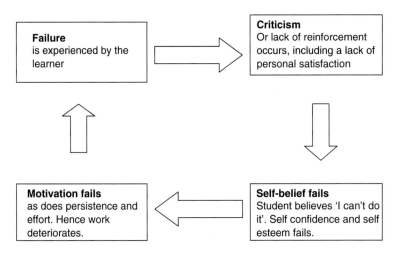

Diagram 3.2 Vicious cycle

Cognitive School

This group of theorists are more interested in the learners' thinking, perception and how they organise their knowledge rather than their behaviours. They argue that the way learners receive information is different according to previous experiences and existing knowledge. Some of the theorists namely Piaget and Kohlberg (Tennant, 1997) argue that learning is developmental. People at different developmental stages process information differently, this is another reason why adults and children learn differently. Cognitivism sees learning as consisting of changes in mental constructs which are ways of representing the world. New learning is linked into existing constructs. The key to learning is understanding, and materials need to be marshalled step by step and then mastered. The enabler could use some of the ideas from this school by presenting new material to previous understandings, for example, using the learners experience of being assessed as learner to help them understand how it feels to be assessed as a parent. They could be encouraged to see that there may be a relationship between how a person copes with the loss of a job and the loss of a loved one. The enabler could facilitate learning by posing specific problems and encouraging the learner to solve them for themselves. The enabler will need to recognise that each learner makes sense of things in their own way and this is influenced by previous experiences.

Social Learning School

This group of theorists argue that learning has a social dimension or context. Individuals within social groups internalise the social norms and values of those groups. Society is a sort of living organism that reproduces itself within its members. It is therefore as important to understand the social context, as it is to understand the psychological mechanism involved in learning. Society requires members to learn social norms and roles in order to survive. However, there is criticism of this functional view of social learning. Jarvis (1987) sees this as presenting a view of individuals as passive recipients of the prevailing cultural values. He argues that individuals actually modify what they receive, and the modified version is transmitted to other people in social interaction. Learning is not seen as social adaptation as in the functionalist model but as social action and interaction. Bandura (Tennant, 1997) argues that individual and environmental influences are interdependent. He considers the importance of modelling and the importance of learning from others. The behaviour of models is more likely to be copied if those models are seen as of a higher status to the learner and if their behaviour gains them socially acceptable recognition in the eyes of the learner. The enabler could utilise some of the ideas from the Social Learning School by remembering that the social context may influence matters such as motivation. What is considered to be a criterion for success on one social group may not be in another. The behaviour of role models are likely to be copied if the model is seen as of a higher status to the learner. So staff with good standing in an agency might be useful to assist with the learning.

Humanist School

This school sees the individual as the most important element of the learning process. It sees the learner as having a desire to grow and develop, and the job of the enabler is to create the environment in which this is possible. These ideas of self-transformation and self-development are at the base of humanistic theories on personality development. Maslow (1986) developed a hierarchy of needs on which he based his model of human development. The needs at the base of the hierarchy such as food and warmth must be met before the individual can consider meeting higher needs such as love and self-esteem. At the top of the hierarchy is the need for self-actualisation. Maslow argues that learning is the way to achieve self-actualisation. Freire (1985) argues that education is not a neutral process; it is either designed to facilitate freedom or to facilitate domestication. If it is to facilitate freedom then the enabler needs to encourage the learner to challenge assumptions and view what he or she is learning with a critical eye. The enabler could use key ideas from this school by ensuring that the learner has his or her basic needs met before starting to learn. Learners should particularly feel safe within the learning environment (see Chapter 2 on Learning Partnership). Learners should wherever possible be encouraged to follow their own interests.

Experiential learning

This model comes out of the humanistic school of learning. It has become quite central to ideas about adult learning. Kolb writing with Fry in 1975 drew up what is perhaps the best-known illustration about learning; the experiential Learning Cycle (see Diagram 3.3). This cycle can start anywhere acknowledging that we can learn both by having a concrete experience ourselves and also from the description of an experience by another. Any experience whether direct or indirect will be filtered through our own autobiography and is therefore individual.

Kolb and Fry claim that once the cycle is started it should be continuous. Jarvis (1987) found the cycle too simple and tested it with a variety of groups of adult learners. The findings of the tests were incorporated into the model and then it was re-tested. A more complex model emerged with a variety of learning routes. Jarvis identified nine types of response to an experience, which he classified into three groups.

Group one is 'Non-learning' where learners fail to learn from the experience because they reject it out of hand or they do not see the need for change or they are fearful of change. Group two is 'Non-reflective Learning' where learners learn but do not analyse the process. They may learn incidentally as when individuals may be able to recall an advertising slogan on a bill board. They may learn to reproduce actions by rote or facts by memorising them. These responses will just reproduce the status quo. Group three is 'Reflective Learning' where responses may include just thinking about the experience without reaching a conclusion, producing new skills and ideas in response to a unique situation or trying out knowledge in practice. Thus, an experience does not always result in formulation of concepts, which are then tested on new situations.

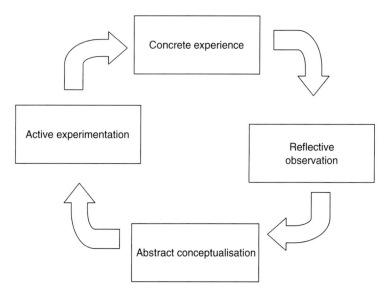

Diagram 3.3 Experiential learning cycle

Practical experience in professional education is one of the most important forms of learning, yet it tends to be missing from the categories of experiential learning. Jarvis (1996) suggests that this is because the practical experience is seen as the application or transfer of learning from the classroom rather than learning itself. This is a misleading idea since learning in the practical situation is learning from primary experience. The learners bring with them learning from all previous experiences, the more they have learned from previous experiences the more likely they are to have some knowledge which they can use in the new situation. If the learner meets a situation for the first time and does not know how to act then this is a learning situation. They will learn from trial and error, observing others, questioning others and then acting. We cannot learn everything from primary experiences. We learn much from the experiences of others through various forms of communication. Learners react to secondary experiences in a similar way to when they encounter primary experiences. A variety of factors will determine whether reflective or non-reflective learning takes place. Much theory is learnt through secondary experience. However, it is difficult to ensure that one theory relates to all situations and by its very nature it must be generalised. Learner must then adapt the theory to the particular situation in which they find themselves. This is particularly true for social work students who need to adapt the knowledge they have acquired in the university to variable workplaces.

Learning to Learn

Lucas (2002) argues that learners need to have an awareness of how they learn in order to become a competent learner. He adopts the term 'learnacy' to explain the concept. He argues that we are all individuals with different preferences and ways of doing things. So people will learn in different ways from one another. He identifies three factors, which influence our learning preferences. These are as follows:

- Where we prefer to learn.
- How we absorb information most easily.
- How we process information once we have absorbed it.

Often we have no choice about where we are learning but given a choice most people would prefer to learn at home or in the workplace. As well as location, other factors are important, such as timing, surroundings, other people and so on.

ACTIVITY

Take a moment to consider your own preferences using the questions below.

Given the choice:

Where would you prefer to learn?

Would you prefer to learn alone or with others?

Would you prefer to learn by doing practical tasks, thinking for yourself, watching others, reading or some other way?

Would you prefer to be quiet or have noise around?

Would you prefer to be at a desk or lounging in a chair?

Do you learn best at night or first thing in a morning or sometime in between?

How warm do you like to be?

Do you prefer to have a supply of food and drink or do without?

Finding out about our preferences can save us time and prevent us thinking that we cannot do something when in fact we could do it if we went about it in a different way.

The next stage is to consider how you prefer to absorb information. Generally, we take in information through our senses. The senses can be grouped into the following.

- Sight (visual learning);
- Hearing (auditory learning);
- Smell, taste and touch (kinaesthetic learning).

Most people prefer one way of absorbing information to others. One way is not better than the others; they are just different. Have you ever been in a meeting specifically to plan new ideas and found that some people automatically reach for the flip chart to represent their views diagrammatically, whereas others just write down words and others may get people to try out the ideas? All are valid ways of trying to absorb new ideas but not everyone is able to use all ways effectively.

If you prefer verbal instruction, remember names, like listening to music, listen to thoughts in your head then you are probably an auditory learner.

If you like maps, remember faces, co-ordinate your appearance and visualise patterns then you are probably a visual learner.

If you prefer to have a go, do more than one thing at once and are expressive with your body then you are probably a kinaesthetic learner.

Marshalling information according to these preferences will assist learning.

Learning Styles

Lucas' last factor is the way in which we deal with information. This is generally known as our learning style. From Kolb's learning cycle comes his idea that there are different styles of learning associated with the four different parts of the cycle. Kolb (1975) is one of many writers to consider that people learn in different ways. There are numerous inventories and questionnaires designed to test in what ways learners learn best. Once this has been ascertained the enabler can design learning programmes with the learners to meet their style, thus developing individual learning packages for each learner. Clearly, this idea is difficult to achieve when dealing with large groups of learners but has considerable appeal for the one to one or small group learning situations, which are common in social work practice.

However, the research on the various instruments used to ascertain learning style indicates that they are not as effective as their designers claim. A literature review by Coffield, Moseley, Hall and Ecclestone (2004) for the Learning and Skills Research Centre found 71 but considered 13 major models of learning styles. They concluded, 'that there was marked variability in quality among them; they are not all alike nor have equal worth and it matters fundamentally which instrument is chosen' (p. 55). Some of the best-known and widely used instruments to ascertain learning styles had serious weaknesses. Only three models were considered to be close to meeting all the criteria of internal consistency, test–retest reliability, construct validity and predictive validity. These were the models of Allison and Hayes (1996), Apter (2001) and Vermunt (1998); a further three, those of Entwhistle et al. (2001) Hermann (1989) and Myers-Briggs and Mc Caulley (1985) met two of the four criteria. The models in common usage in the United Kingdom for social work education: Honey and Mumford (1996) and Kolb (1999) and the Dunn and Dunn (2003) models that are popular in the United States of America met only one criterion each.

This literature review indicates a lack of vigorous testing of the learning styles inventories and models. The authors found inflated claims and sweeping conclusions, which went beyond the current knowledge base about the models. Yet the concept of learning styles is one which holds favour within the field of adult education. This is possibly because many practitioners have discovered for themselves that the traditional method of transmission of information by the teacher and assimilation by the student fails to work for many students. The learning style literature provides a possible explanation for this failure and some ideas for a resolution. The idea that educators need to find the key to unlock each learner's potential rather than use a 'one style fits all' approach can transform their attitude to learners who they may previously have seen as lazy, slow or stupid.

Much of the work on learning styles indicates that they are relatively fixed and stable over time so that they can be defined accurately and measured reliably through psychological tests. This has not been proven by reliable research. These ideas can lead to labelling which can in turn become predictive. It also requires that teaching should be offered to match the learner's style which is not always possible. Another idea flowing from the concept of learning styles is that they can be used to encourage students to be more self aware of their own strengths and weaknesses. They can then play to their strengths and work on their weaknesses. Other educators promote the idea that learners should be encouraged to develop a repertoire of styles in order to be able to take advantage of learning offered in a variety of ways. Similarly, they suggest that enablers should offer learning in a variety of styles to meet the needs of different types of learner.

Although Coffield et al. (2004) are critical of Honey and Mumford's learning styles questionnaire they do acknowledge that they offer helpful strategies to encourage learners to develop their less predominant learning styles. A visit to Peter Honey's website (www.peterhoney.com) will enable the visitor (for a fee) to ascertain his or her own learning style and to download a series of suggestions for developing other styles. According to Coffield et al. (2004) the popular recommendation coming out of learning style work is that the learning styles of learners should be linked to the teaching styles of the enabler. Yet the studies which they considered covering this area were contradictory. Matching may help performance initially but it does nothing to prepare learners for situations they may meet where styles do not match.

The popularity in social work education of the concept of learning styles cannot be denied. Most candidates doing practice teacher training through the General Social Care Council (GSCC) approved course have undertaken some form of learning styles questionnaire, usually Honey and Mumford (Cartney, 2000). Many are captivated by the idea and see it as a tool to enable them to pitch learning in a way which suits the learner best. However, Cartney (2000) discovered that although practice teachers (enablers) generally used learning styles questionnaires, they did not utilise the information to inform the student's learning process. One of her conclusions is that practice teachers need to be given more explicit information about how to use the knowledge gained from the learning styles questionnaires.

In view of the work of both Coffield et al. (2004) and Cartney (2000) it is probably more useful to consider some of the ideas of learning styles and their implication rather than to rely heavily on the questionnaires to identify specific styles. Perhaps the simplest way of identifying a probable preference for one learning style over another is to ask a potential learner how he or she would prefer to learn something new.

Learners who are aware of their own learning style can direct their own learning in ways which maximise on this knowledge. Enablers need to be aware of their own learning preferences as well as those of the learner as learning style can influence enabling style.

You probably found that in some situations you could quite happily

---

ACTIVITY

Both learners and enablers alike can do the exercise below as a quick way to ascertain their own learning style.

If you had to find you way to a new destination would you prefer to do the following.

- Look at a map?
- Ask someone for direction?
- Ask someone to take you?
- Find a bus going in the direction required and follow it?
- Set of in the general direction and see if you can find it?

If you had to master the use of a new gadget would you prefer to do the following.

- Read the manual?
- Ask someone (preferably a teenager) to demonstrate what it can do?
- Figure it out from previous experience of similar things?
- Just have a go?

Do your answers vary depending on the following.

- What sort of new learning is required?
- Previous experience with similar learning?

---

learn in any of the ways suggested, but in another situation only one way would be effective depending on your prior experience and abilities. For example, if you have a good sense of direction and are not frightened of being in unfamiliar areas then you could probably find a new place by just setting off in the general direction. If you are more anxious about unfamiliar places and have no sense of direction you may need a map. If you are a technophobe then having a go with a new gadget will not get you anywhere. Use the exercise above to ask members of your family (use a range of ages) and your colleagues for their preferences. This will hopefully show you the differences amongst people in the way they prefer to learn.

Learning new things or trying to apply existing knowledge in new settings can cause the learner to become anxious. In order to reduce anxiety and not inhibit learning it is useful to start enabling learning in the style of the learners' preference, providing this is feasible. This is more likely to achieve success, which will then build their confidence and reduce anxiety. Later when learners are more settled and more confident, it is probably useful to encourage them to experiment with different styles to extend their repertoire and ensure that they can learn in a variety of situations. The enabler can ascertain styles of preference by asking questions similar to those in the exercises above. Many students may arrive to undertake work-based learning having already completed one of the learning styles questionnaires mentioned above. It is worth checking the questionnaire to see that you understand their preferences and how best to meet those preferences.

Research by Entwhistle (1996) and others indicate that when faced with a task such as reading a text, students will approach it in different ways depending on their purpose for the task. Entwhistle considered two approaches: the surface approach and the deep approach. In the surface approach, the learner memorises the facts and remembers the things which are emphasised, they are concerned about remembering the content and being able to reproduce the information unchanged. In the deep approach the learner tries to make sense of the information, looks for patterns and meaning. They consider whether the evidence is valid and whether or not the arguments are logical and justify the conclusions reached. They link new information to existing ideas. Entwhistle discovered that these approaches are not personal but context dependent. The same person undertaking different learning tasks or working in different circumstances can use both approaches. Learners who wish to meet course requirements for one particular task may well adopt a surface approach, for example if they need to pass a law exam. They may consider that the knowledge is not likely to be of long-term use or is too complex to understand. They may also be anxious and fear failure, therefore, prefer to reproduce information verbatim rather than risk getting something wrong. The surface approach means that learning is not retained for long and is not linked to related concepts but kept isolated. It is fine provided a critical understanding of the knowledge is not required. It is unlikely to lead to a change of views or understanding. Learners who wish to understand ideas for themselves will use a deep approach. They reorganise existing knowledge to accommodate new knowledge. There is a sense of things 'clicking into place'. They will be able to reproduce an account of their new knowledge, which is integrated with other ideas and so consolidated into a coherent whole. New knowledge may lead to changes in views and understanding. Entwhistle refers to strategic learners as those people who can adapt their approach depending on the learning task. These learners are the ones who can be the most effective learners.

ACTIVITY

Explore Entwhistle's ideas in your own workplace. You will then be in a position to encourage the learner to be strategic.

Think of some things which a learner new to your work base would need to know but could use a surface approach to learn. For example, the areas of a service user's life which are considered in an assessment.

Think of some things which a learner new to your work base would need to know but would need to adopt a deep approach to learn. For example, How the information gathered in an assessment is used to make a recommendation.

Enabler Styles

It seems that there is a correlation between an individual's learning style and the way in which they enable learning in others (Coffield et al., 2004; Cartney, 2000). If the learner who arrives in the workplace has a different style to the enabler, then there is a possibility of misunderstanding if the enabler does not recognise this. Consider learners who like to think through a plan of action before doing anything, matched with enablers who like to get cracking and think on their feet. Without a consideration of their differences the enabler may think the learner slow or reluctant to undertake a task. This could have repercussions for any further work, which is given to the learner and to the judgements made about the learner's competence. The key seems to be to discuss learning styles and preferences of enablers and learners right at the start of any work-based learning.

There are other factors which have an influence on enabler style. The first is the enabler's belief about his or her role in the learning process. There are questionnaires which will help ascertain the enabler's view, notably Bartram and Gibson (1993) who look at trainers, and Reece and Walker (2000) who consider teachers. They are based on finding the respondent's position on a continuum of belief, which has at one end the following assumptions:

- People need to be made to learn.
- The facilitator is the most important person in the learning process.
- It is the facilitator's job to decide how learning should take place.
- The facilitator should be an expert in his or her field.
- The facilitator makes judgements about the learner's abilities and knows best how things should be learnt.
- Learning takes place when the facilitator is passing on his or her expertise.
- People learn best by listening, copying and watching experts.

At the other end of the continuum the assumptions would be the following.

- People enjoy learning for its own sake.
- People know what they need to learn, so should be in control of their own learning environment.
- Learners must take responsibility for their own learning.
- The experiences of the learner are as valid as those of the facilitator.
- Learners know their own strengths and weaknesses best and how they prefer to learn.
- Learning can take place at any time and in any situation.
- People learn best by doing and considering the consequences of their actions.

Consider where you would be on the continuum. The top set are linked to teacher/trainer-centred learning. The bottom set are linked to student-centred learning or facilitation. You may find that you do not feel affinity to one set of statements and want to say to yourself that it depends on the situation and the level of experience of the learner in relation to the subject under consideration. This leads us to consider Heron's view (Heron, 1989) that the enabler may use different modes of facilitation (or enabling) in different circumstances. He refers to three modes:

1. The hierarchical mode where the enabler decides on the learning programme, interprets and gives meaning, challenges resistance and manages feelings. Generally enablers provide the structures for the learning and take full charge of all the decisions of the learning process.
2. The co-operative mode where there is a sharing of the power in the learning process. The enabler prompts the learner to decide on the learning programme. The enabler's view is influential but not final.
3. The autonomous mode where the enabler respects the total autonomy of the learner. The basis of the learning is that it is self-directed. The enabler's role is to create the conditions in which people can take responsibility for their own learning.

ACTIVITY

Use the exercise below to help you utilise all the information included in the chapter so far to provide learning in the most effective way for the learner.

Think about two very different people who may come to your workplace to learn the same thing, for example, completing an initial referral or recording admission information.

Learner A is an experienced home care assistant who has worked across a range of service user groups and is used to making reports to her manager on the needs of the people with whom she works.

Learner B is someone who has recently left Sixth Form College; she volunteered during her spare time in a project providing food and clothing to homeless people.

What might you need to know about each learner before you made any decisions about your enabling style/mode?

How might you adapt your style of enabling to match the needs of each learner?

Blocks to Learning

Some learners have positive experiences of learning, feel confident of their ability to acquire new knowledge and skills given the right support and come to work-based learning eager and open to learn. These learners have frequently done well in the education system and devised effective personal strategies to facilitate their learning. Others have poor experiences of formal education which means that they have labelled themselves (or even been labelled by others) as stupid and come to work-based learning anxious and lacking in confidence. When doing an exercise with adult learners about their experiences of school, we are always struck by the significant number of them who found the whole experience of school traumatic. They have had their experience of learning blighted by teachers, parents or significant others who condemned them because they could not learn in the same way or time as their classmates. Anxiety inhibits learning and the label becomes a self-fulfilling prophecy, the learner is blocked by anxiety.

Other factors can create anxiety for learners and block their learning. Adult learners often have responsibilities outside the learning environment such as caring for dependants. If they are students learning in a placement they may not have the capacity to alter their support systems to give them full cover during that learning experience. They have probably set up their systems to cope with the hours they are normally in university. They will have to make new arrangements which need to be tried and tested. Initial anxiety about whether or not the arrangements will work may be enough to inhibit learning. Concern from the enabler about the learner as a whole person with a willingness to be flexible, and reassurance that the learner's worries are taken seriously may well help to remove this sort of block to learning.

Previous experiences of learning may well have been primarily teacher-centred and the idea of being responsible for one's own learning could be difficult to contemplate with learners always seeking the 'right' way of working with the enabler and not being able to develop their own style. Most degree and post-qualification programmes in social work include student-centred activities such as problems-based learning, group discussions and projects. These will have prepared learners for a range of different ideas about service users' lives and how to work with them. When learners move into the workplace the enabler might encourage them to see various workers in action doing the same sort of task. They can then discuss the advantages of the different methods with the learner before setting a rehearsal of how the learner might undertake the task for themselves.

Morrison (2001) uses Kolb's learning cycle to consider other learning blocks. He recognises that learners can become stuck in one phase of the learning cycle which prevents them from moving round the cycle and utilising their experiences to formulate ideas and develop their practice. He identifies two forms of block, the first being people who become blocked because of a particular situation, the second being that they are blocked in a more endemic way, which is a result of their personality. Morrison argues that once the block has been identified action can be taken to unblock the process.

Consider Jo who is unable to see things from another's point of view and is unaware of the impact he has on service users and other colleagues. He is unable to step back from a situation and be analytical. He works in what he considers to be the right way without any use of theory or objective evidence. He tends to procrastinate and seems unable to complete tasks. He is preoccupied with himself and is blocked at reflection. Strategies to unblock persons stuck in reflection centre around encouraging them to undertake small tasks. This will build their confidence that they can actually achieve something. So the main task needs to be split into manageable proportions, they need to understand the expectations required of them. The task needs to be within their capability, or training needs to be provided. Links can be made to similar tasks, which they have successfully achieved previously and they can be encouraged to transfer ideas from one task to another. Time limits can be set with feedback given at each stage. After the task is completed they can be helped to analyse what they did well and areas to improve.

Nasreen similarly has poor empathy; she avoids emotions and focuses on the task rather than the process. She tends to intellectualise and use theory to justify inaction. She generally works alone with little co-operation to others. Nasreen is scathing when discussing colleagues who she sees as too involved with the people that they are working with, she is blocked at analysis. Strategies to unblock the person stuck in analysis include concentrating on the feelings and process in any interaction, avoiding generalisations and focusing on the specifics of the issue in question. Enablers working with this block should avoid entering intellectual debates about the issue.

Robert on the other hand tends to overidentify with service users, he rushes around doing things that he considers service users need or want without discussing it with them first. He cannot give a rationale for his actions except to infer that he knows best. He has poor boundaries and has become overinvolved with service users visiting them in his own time. He is resistant to challenges and unable to reflect on the impact of his own performance. Robert is blocked at action. Strategies to unblock in this situation include maintaining clear boundaries as the enabler, asking for summaries of the work they are doing with rationale for intervention. They will probably need help with time management and the setting of priorities. Conversely Susanne seems to avoid contact with service users. She seems unmoved by even the direst situations. She is an experienced worker and is resistant to new ideas claiming that they have been tried before. Her work tends to be routine or superficial, she reacts to situations, taking up issues she discovers from other professionals rather than planning her work. Suzanne is blocked at experiencing. Strategies to unblock this process need to concentrate not only on both care for the individual but also on their accountability for the work, which they are undertaking. Morrison suggests two possible causes for this block which may be 'burn-out' or trauma. Suzanne is cynical and negative, probably suffering from overload in the past. The traumatised worker is more likely to be fearful and diffident. Strategies to unblock the learning involve clarification of the learners' perceptions of their role and responsibility, and checking out their feelings about their work. Learners who are traumatised may need specialised help to cope. Helping learners to overcome a learning block can mean that they are in a position to move forward and improve their practice and thus the service they offer. Recognition of the block is the key and can prevent them being 'written off' as difficult individuals who can't or won't learn.

Key Learning Points

- People take in and process information in different ways.
- Learning how we and others learn can increase the effectiveness of learning strategies and can prevent learners thinking that they cannot do something when in fact they could do it if they were enabled differently.

- The various schools of learning theories have important factors which can be applied to learning in the workplace but no one theory explains all aspects of learning.
- Past experiences of learning can impact on our attitude and ability in new learning situations.
- Learners can become stuck or blocked at stages in their learning and may need.

CHAPTER 4

Creating and Using Learning Opportunities

This chapter will consider how to identify the learning needs of individuals using the National Occupational Standards (NOS) as a base, and how opportunities can be provided to enable learners to meet their needs and demonstrate competence in key roles. Enablers working with PQ learners will need to use both these standards and those relating to PQ skills and knowledge. 'In the practice setting, there are considerable opportunities to learn from a well constructed workload and from other staff, without explicit teaching from a designated practice teacher' (Evans, 1999, p. 32).

Although true, this statement fails to consider learners who may need initial help to develop the knowledge and skills necessary before they can take advantage of the learning opportunities available. Similarly, it does not acknowledge the greater awareness learners can gain from a learning opportunity when they have a skilled enabler to guide them.

Learners on educational programmes leading either to a degree or a post qualifying (PQ) award in social work will gain knowledge and ideas through the teaching within the university. The staff in these institutions are generally working together with several learners who have very mixed experiences and levels of existing knowledge and skills. The learners will need to be prepared for a general rather than a specific social work role, as the specifics are too numerous to be considered. Lecturers thus need to provide knowledge which can be utilised by all the learners. It will therefore be general and broad-based. The learner and the enabler in the workplace then need to work to make this general knowledge particular to that setting. For example, most syllabi will include different theories and models of assessment, but most social work settings use a method of assessment, which is adapted to their needs.

Social work degree programmes need to produce graduates who are fit for purpose, that is, that they can work as social workers. Students need to be clear about the social work value base and how it differs from that of other professions, so that they can define their own professional identity and boundaries (Parker, 2004). In designing the social work degree, universities were cognisant of guidance and requirements issued by the Department of Health, The General Social Care Council (GSCC) and the Quality Assurance Agency. PQ programmes have developed based on the GSCC PO requirements (GSCC, 2005). Each university will have interpreted these requirements and guidance slightly differently. They will introduce students to theories and models which can be classified according to three types (Payne, 1991). Those which will help them make sense of what social work is; those which help make sense of the situations of service users and those which guide their actions when working with them. Each social work education programme will place a different emphasis on the type of theory and then again within each type. So learners coming to practice from different social work education programmes may have differences in their knowledge base. Also the way universities package the required 200 days of placement across years of the degree programme varies enormously in length, number and position within the degree. Consequently, it is important for the enabler to be familiar with the programme of study on which the learner is placed. Thus the role of the lecturer or tutor within the university is to develop knowledge and ideas within the learner, whereas the enabler in the workplace has the role of helping the learner use and adapt this knowledge to best effect in that particular workplace. Discussion with other learners back in university will throw up differences in practice which can be explored further with the university staff. This then helps the learners develop skills in transferring knowledge across settings and analytical skills that will be invaluable as they move into different agencies and roles.

Learners on qualifying programmes for one of the caring professions generally consider that the practice placement or learning in the work base is *the* most important contribution to their learning. There is some evidence that satisfaction with the enabler in this practice setting is the best predictor for satisfaction of the whole experience (Fernandez, 1998; Macleod, Clarke et al., 1996; Walker et al., 1995).

All practitioners in social work are familiar with the requirement to assess the needs of service users in order to identify their individual requirements and plan a package of care to meet these requirements.

They are also aware that this package needs regular review in light of the changing needs and circumstances of the service user. The situation is exactly the same for learners, whatever their stage of professional development. Some assessment is required of what they need to learn; a plan needs to be constructed to facilitate learning and the plan needs continual monitoring and reviewing in order to see whether or not they are learning.

Learning Outcomes

Learning outcomes or learning objectives are the standards that the learners are expected to meet. Learning needs are the identified gaps in a learner's knowledge, skills and application of values and attitudes. Learning needs are individual in that they depend on previous experiences and previous learning. An individual's learning needs includes the following:

- new knowledge and skills
- an understanding of the values which underpin their work together with
- a revision of existing knowledge and skills which may need to be applied in new circumstances.

If the learner is on a recognised educational programme there will be specified learning outcomes identified by that programme. In terms of national professional or vocational qualifications these will be prescribed through NOS. The White Paper 'Working Together – Education and Training' (1986) set the task to establish new standards of performance for all areas of British industry because the government was concerned about capabilities of the British workforce in comparison with that of other EU partners. The progress made in each occupational area was vastly different and it wasn't until 2002/2003 that the standards were set for social work. These were written by the Training Organisation for the Personal Social Services (TOPSS), since replaced by separate training organisations for staff working with children (Children's Workforce Development Council) and those working with adults (Skills for Care). TOPSS drew together groups of representatives from various agencies within social work to collaborate on the standards. This approach has two obvious advantages and one main disadvantage:

> It opens up to public inspection the thinking behind the specification
> of objectives, whilst the inclusion of representatives of key interests
> in the process increases the chances of their findings being widely
> accepted ... issues may at times be fudged by the need to comprom-
> ise, and findings may be reduced to the common denominator
> underlying a variety of different perceptions. (Melton, 1997, p. 12)

As is the case with other competencies, the NOS for social work
indicate what workers should be able to do in order to demonstrate
that they have met the standards set. The competence approach tries to
be as objective as possible but by its very nature social work is not
scientific but involves human judgements which vary according to the
individuals making them. The standards are open to interpretation by
those using them. They consist of broad statements of key functions or
roles within social work as practised across a range of settings. There
are six key roles in total. Functional analysis was employed to identify
what workers must be able to do in order for the key roles to be performed across a range of settings. The analysis was completed in a
series of stages with the levels of performance becoming increasingly
more detailed and explicit at each stage. The key roles are thus split
down into 21 units which are again subdivided into 77 elements of
competence. Each element is then expanded into performance criteria.
To achieve an element of competence, learners should be able to
demonstrate that they can do everything that is spelt out through the
performance criteria. This can lead to a concentration on the minutia
and a loss of appreciation of the whole because the whole is often
greater than the sum of its parts. Dominelli (1996) argues that it is a
dogmatic and inflexible approach which reduces complex social interactions to snapshots, and moves away from relationship building which
is the fundamental core of the profession. Inputs and process are not of
interest in the model which is focused on short-term goals of getting
people to do specific tasks not to challenge the system. Early definitions
of competence concentrated on required performance in any job. The
specification of knowledge seemed to be avoided as though those who
were identifying requirements frightened that knowledge would
become required for its own sake rather than as a means to an end
(Melton, 1997). This led to a great debate in social work education in
the early 1990s about whether a competence-based framework could

be applied to the complexities of the profession. The debate seems to have died down as the government drives the agenda, but the issues have not been resolved.

Later definitions of competence, particularly the NOS for social work, include a range of knowledge which learners must know, understand and be able to critically evaluate and apply in practice. There are a variety of types of knowledge which are classified by writers in different ways (see Bloom, 1956 and Eraut, 1994). Knowledge underpins and is integral to competence. Failure to acquire the knowledge, which, informs competence, could lead to robotic performance with little understanding and poor ability to justify actions and predict outcomes. The learner who has a greater depth of the knowledge of concepts, theories and principles which underpins competence, is more likely to be able to transfer his or her competence to new areas and be able to work within a changing situation (Melton, 1997).

The NOS in social work are thus the learning outcomes which each learner must meet in order to demonstrate his or her competence as a social worker irrespective of the setting in which he or she is working. Thus the NOS could be said to set the framework for any practice learning opportunity provided for learners on a professional social work programme. PQ programmes have in addition specialist standards which they need to incorporate. All these standards are designed to meet the needs of the profession rather than the needs of the individual. An effective enabler of learning must learn to juggle the needs of the individual and the needs of the profession. Learners will need to be able to identify with learning outcomes and feel that they are achievable. Motivation is likely to be increased if they can set their own learning outcomes, but with prescribed standards this is not always possible. The key skill for the enabler when using prescribed standards is to respond flexibly so as not to lose the needs of the individual learner in the process. Enablers themselves may feel de-motivated if learning outcomes are too prescriptive and externally imposed. Realising that it is their responsibility to develop the opportunities and teaching strategies from which the learner can learn and demonstrate competence against the standards can help them recover their motivation.

Sometimes learners have learning needs which are personal and do not necessarily relate to the learning outcomes prescribed by NOS, for example, they may wish to be able to understand basic British Sign Language (BSL) or have an in-depth understanding of a particular medical condition which causes disability. These learning needs are likely to be particularly significant to the individual, and to ignore them may inhibit their learning in other areas. To concentrate solely on them may mean that the learner cannot demonstrate competence in all required areas. Thus, there is a balance to be struck when identifying learning needs between those which are personal to the individual and those which are specific to the educational programme they are undertaking.

ACTVITY

Identifying learning needs

Using the learning outcome from the NOS 'be able to act as an advocate for a service user' (Key Role 3 Unit 10), answer the question below to identify a learner's needs. If you do not have a particular learner in mind you could use yourself to see how it might work.

Identify the small steps involved in the task of acting as an advocate to a service user.

You may have identified some of the following:

- Develop a rapport with the service user using appropriate communication skills.
- Ascertain the views/wants of the service user.
- Gather sufficient information and evaluate key points to prepare a case for advocacy.
- Prepare a case that represents the best interests of the service user.
- Explain clearly and appropriately the procedures, practices and likely outcomes the service user can expect.
- Present the case on behalf of the individual.
- Communicate the outcomes in a way which can be understood.
- Record the results according to legal and organisational procedures.

Once you have identified the steps in the process you will need to identify the knowledge skills and experience required to undertake the task. The learning needs will be the gap between what is required for the task and the knowledge and skills which the learner already possesses.

ACTIVITY

Use the following steps to identify the learning needs in relation to advocacy.

STEP ONE
Identify the knowledge, skills and experience required to undertake an advocacy role. For example, theories in relation to advocacy, types of advocacy, communication skills, principles of empowerment, understanding of agency policies and procedures in relation to advocacy, writing skills, presentation skills, recording skills and having experience of presenting the needs of another.

STEP TWO
Identify which of the knowledge, skills and experience you have listed in step one the learner already possesses at the appropriate level for the task.

STEP THREE
Identify the knowledge, skills and experience the learner already possesses but not at a high enough level.

STEP FOUR
Identify which of the knowledge, skills and experience listed in step one the learner does not possess at all.

Once you have done what is described in the Activity Box you will be able to identify the learning needs of the individual, provide a practice curriculum (see later in chapter) to meet these needs and assess their competence.

Learning Opportunities and Standards

It is important for enablers to recognise that they are not the only source of learning for the learner in the work base. They can provide learning opportunities through other people and even through other work settings. Durkin and Shergill (2000) argue for a team approach to practice teaching or learning. They think that there are considerable benefits for the team, the service users, the student and the practice teacher (enabler) when the whole team is involved in the learning. The contribution of other team members can benefit the student in a greater proportion than the sum of the individual inputs. They argue for careful preparation giving the learner time to adapt to the team as they are an outsider joining an established group. The enabler and learner both need to be clear about who is in the team and how they are going to be involved. The team approach exposes the learner to a range of professional perspectives, strengths and styles of working. Where possible learners should be able to undertake joint work with different members of the team. This will allow them to take various levels of responsibility in working with service users whilst other workers keeps overall accountability for the work. This is an opportunity for the learner to plan and lead discrete sessions within a safe environment. PQ learners will not be new to the team but will be trying to develop new knowledge and skills within their workplace, and so will need to be given special consideration. It will need to be clear when they are learners and when they are undertaking their own job. This has important consequences for accountability. Learners are expected to make mistakes and learn from them. This is not expected of people undertaking their usual job roles.

Thus the enabler is responsible for managing the process of learning for the learner and co-ordinating all the learning opportunities. Adults learn best when they set their own goals, have responsibility for their own learning and are involved in negotiation about their learning. Adult learners can become frustrated and resistant to learning when they are asked to cover things which they can already do (Gibbs, 1995; Rogers, 1969). So it is important that enabler and learner work together to jointly identify the areas where a learner is already proficient and those where further learning and development is needed. Although a time consuming and complex process, it is probably advisable for the enabler and the learner to familiarise themselves with the NOS for social work in order to decide what they actually mean and how they would know whether or not they have been met.

ACTIVITY

Use the exercise below to help you identify opportunities for learning within your work base.

Think about your own work base and make a list of the areas of work which are undertaken by social work staff in that base, for example assessing needs of service users, participating in multidisciplinary meeting, writing formal reports and so on.

These areas of work are part of the learning opportunities which learners can use in order to demonstrate their competence. When you have completed your list try to link the areas of work to the key roles as shown in the table below. This activity can be used if the learner is on a PQ award using those learning outcomes.

Key role	Type of work available in my work base
1. Prepare for and work with individuals, families, groups and communities to assess their needs and circumstance.	
2. Plan, carry out, review and evaluate social work practice with individuals, families, groups, communities and other professionals.	
3. Support individuals to represent their needs, views and circumstances.	
4. Assess risk to individuals, families, groups, communities, self and colleagues.	
5. Manage and be accountable with supervision and support for your own social work practice within your organisation.	For example, supervision sessions, completion of agency document-ation and audit trails and so on.
6. Reflect on and continue to develop your professional practice.	Supervision sessions, case discussions, agency training, other training and so on.

Now that you have completed the exercise given in the table you may wish to look in detail at the gaps in the table. It may be that your work base is one team or service within a wider agency and that some of the gaps can be filled through learning opportunities in other areas of your own agency. So, for example, you may work in a drop in centre for vulnerable young people where you make an assessment of their needs. This results in a referral to a drug awareness programme in another project in your agency. You also contact a housing association for accommodation but maintain contact with the young person for help in maintaining the tenancy and general support. Facilitating the student to follow work through with other teams or agencies involved could fill the gaps you have identified in learning opportunities available in your own team. This would require careful management, but it is possible. If you are in the private, voluntary or independent sector linking with statutory agencies may give the learner opportunities which enhance those available in your service and vice versa. Some voluntary and independent agencies have a series of separate projects each providing specific opportunities. Arrangements for a student to work across projects could mean that the range of opportunities available is sufficient to meet all key roles.

So, consider the gaps again and think whether or not they could be overcome by providing learning opportunities in services that are closely linked with your own. For more detail about what is included in any key role you should look at both units and performance criteria to give a more concise picture of what is required in order to demonstrate competence. You may need to distinguish between general learning opportunities which thread through the whole of the practice curriculum, for example, recording information appropriate to an assessment and learning opportunities which are specific to a particular service area. The latter may be the only time for the learner to experience this particular opportunity, for example, attending an adoption panel.

ACTIVITY

List the learning opportunities which may be specific to your area of work and those which are non-specific.

Learning opportunities of a general nature	Learning opportunities which are specific to my work base
For example, undertaking an assessment and recording information	For example, providing victim awareness courses|

This will allow you and a learner to understand what is special about your setting. Most social work degree programmes will have linked certain key roles to a particular level of study and/or placement in some way. It is important that you know what is expected of students at each level so that you can identify for which level of placement/s your work base can offer learning opportunities. Some work bases will be able to offer learning opportunities which allow learners to meet all competencies; others will be more restrictive in the opportunities which they can offer. For example in Key Role 2, Unit 8 learners have to demonstrate their competence in planning and running groups for service users. Some agencies do not use group work as a tool but could allow students to extend the agency repertoire by developing groups. Others may not be able or willing to offer this learning opportunity. It is important to be clear about what can be offered so that realistic and achievable goals can be set. 'In order to make effective use of a new learning situation, learners will need to know what can be learned in a particular placement' (Hinchliff, 1999 p. 85).

Planning a Practice Curriculum

Using the competence identified earlier about acting as an advocate to a service user we can think about the practice curriculum required to enable the learner to develop knowledge, skills and apply values so that they demonstrate competence in this area. The learning opportunities to assist them might include the following.

- Observing different people undertaking the role of advocate.
- Undertaking reading about the role of an advocate and theories of advocacy.
- Spending time with different service users and finding out about their views and wants.
- Reading cases prepared by others acting as advocate.
- Undertaking joint work with an experienced advocate where the roles of both are clearly spelt out.
- Role-playing the presentation of the case and communicating the outcomes.
- Reading the recordings made by experienced advocates.
- Writing their own recording of a case to compare with that written by the experienced advocates.

The number of these learning opportunities utilised will depend on the existing level of knowledge and skill of the learner. At each stage they will need feedback on their performance and the opportunity to discuss their plans and to test out ideas with their enabler. Thus, providing opportunities is not sufficient to enable learning, but supervision and reflection should be included to enable the learner to make the most of the learning opportunities offered.

In the example above it could be that your agency uses a specialist advocacy service. In this case it might be possible for the specialist service to take the learner for a short period of time to give them concentrated experiences in this area. The enabler would need to identify a specific person in the specialist service with whom they can liaise. They must be clear about the learning outcomes the learner needs to demonstrate and how these will be assessed. Delegation of learning opportunities to other people is not an easy option. It requires careful planning and preparation if it is to be useful. The more exposure learners have to the working practices of others the more material they have on which to base their own practice. Learners will need to discuss the strengths and weaknesses of different approaches and reflect on what they have observed in order to decide which approaches are the most appropriate in which circumstances. Thus it is important for the enabler to continue to be involved when learning opportunities are provided elsewhere, as it is the enabler who has oversight of all the learner's needs.

The enabler should remember to consider the learner's learning style in order to start with the type of learning strategy to which they respond best. This will make them feel confident initially. Different strategies can be introduced to stretch them later when they are confident of the basic requirements for any specific task. Undertaking the sort of tasks outlined above will give evidence towards other units and elements as well. The more familiar the enabler becomes with the roles, units, elements and performance criteria the easier it will be for them to identify developing competencies.

Marsick and Watkins (1990) distinguish between informal learning and incidental learning. The former they define as planned, usually experiential, including self-directed learning, coaching and mentoring. Incidental learning is considered to be unplanned and usually a by-product of another activity. The difficulty with incidental learning is that what people learn in this way may not be inherently correct or what the enabler wishes them to learn. The incidental learner may learn that cutting corners is actually advantageous to the worker as this gives them more time to do other things. They may not then be around to see the consequences of the corner taking for the service user. Incidental learning cannot be prevented. To ensure that it is used to the best advantage, it helps if the learner can be encouraged to surface their tacit theories and beliefs. When these are in the open the enabler can work with them to bring about change. Again this illustrates the importance of supervision and reflection on learning that is taking place within the work base. Learning is enhanced when individuals are proactive by seeking out new learning experiences and opportunities.

Jarvis and Gibson (1997) argue that it is an effective use of time to undertake an appraisal of where a student is at before providing learning opportunities. The learner and enabler should jointly identify areas where a learner is already proficient and those where further learning is needed. This is particularly important where adult learners are concerned as they learn best when involved in the process and can see the point of what they are learning. Once this diagnosis is made the leaner and enabler work together to create what Jarvis and Gibson (1997) call the 'negotiated curriculum'. They stress that negotiation should be an ongoing process. The use of the term implies that it is a deliberate process that considers the key areas a learner must learn.

Teaching and Learning Strategies

Once the learning needs have been established and a negotiated curriculum devised consideration should be given to the teaching and learning strategies most appropriate for each particular learner. These will depend on the subject area under consideration, the learning style of the learner, the enabler's style and resources available. Some enabler styles have been considered previously (Chapter 3) and to add to these Jarvis and Gibson (1997) consider three styles which are listed below:

- The *didactic style* where the enabler gives out information, and the learner being seen as an empty vessel.
- The *Socratic style* where the enabler sees the learner as an active thinker already having some knowledge which can be pulled out of them by the use of questions. In effect, the enabler sets problems for the learner to solve.
- The *facilitative style* whereby the enabler sets the conditions under which learning takes place and then steps back to allow the learner to learn; the enabler being available to be used as a resource by the learner.

At different points in providing a practice curriculum the enabler may operate in different styles. However much of a learning climate is created learners will not learn unless they have some basic knowledge and skills on which to build. It may be that in areas completely new to the learner the enabler will have to use a didactic style initially. After this enablers may change to the Socratic style to satisfy themselves that learners have gained and understood the knowledge they need before undertaking a specific task or piece of work. This is particularly appropriate when working with people where the idea of just having a go to see what happens could lead to dire consequences.

Some of the teaching/learning techniques which an enabler may use will include all of the following. Observation: where the learner observes the practice of several workers undertaking the same sort of task, for example, completing an initial assessment. This gives the learner a range of different approaches to the same task to consider. The enabler then discusses with learners the various merits of the different approaches and helps them consolidate their own approach. Inputs of information may be particularly important for learners who are embarking on areas where they have limited or no knowledge. Depending on learner preference this may be given in written, diagrammatic or aural form. It is important to remember that attention spans can be short and so lengthy inputs can produce diminishing returns. Planning will ensure that the information is given in a logical and coherent way. It is probably better that the person giving the input is good at explaining things rather than eminently knowledgeable in his or her subject. Discussions are useful to elicit the knowledge and understanding of the learner if the enabler is asking the questions. If the learner is asking the questions then they can use them to supplement their existing knowledge. A combination of questions from both enabler and learner probably works best. In this way the key issues for the learner will surface and the enabler will be able to ensure that all important areas are considered. Discussions are particularly important to help the learner identify theory and research which will underpin their practice. Role play or skill rehearsal can be used to help learners gain experience of a specific role or the view point of another. It is important that the role play or skill rehearsal is considered and analysed. These methods allow practice in a safe environment. They have been criticised because they can be seen as artificial, the emphasis being on the performance rather than the experience. Enablers who value these techniques themselves as learning tools are more likely to be able to persuade reluctant learners of their value. Debriefing is an important part of the process. Learners can play the role of the practitioner to gain expertise or the role of the service user to gain understanding and empathy with their position. It requires careful supervision, as emotions and attitudes may surface which are not expected, and the enabler should be in a position to deal with these. Case studies which use real or fictitious situations can help students think through how people may be feeling, what they can do as practitioners and what resources they may need. These can take the form of written work or discussions in supervision. Assignments/projects or small pieces of research whereby the learner investigates a need or the views of service users or undertakes a piece of work to improve the service offered by an agency (see below). Spider diagrams or mind maps, and diagrams which include all the knowledge which a learner needs to bring to bear in any particular situation are useful to identify the knowledge in order to ensure that the learner has got it. If there are gaps in the learner's knowledge, for example, in terms of theory which might explain behaviour or the legal aspects of the situation, remedial action can be taken. Joint working where learners can work with a range of colleagues within a team as well as the enabler can assist a worker with, for example, undertaking a joint assessment. This will allow them to take some responsibility in a safe environment. Or, as they get more proficient, they can undertake discrete pieces of work with service users and carers as part of an overall plan of work. This will give them more responsibility for the work, but someone else keeps overall accountability. This can help build confidence for a learner. Taking responsibility for a complete piece of work with a service user will allow learners to develop their own method of working and demonstrate competence. This is clearly important if they are about to qualify as a professional or take on new responsibilities in the workplace. However, if they are on lower levels of practice experience this may not be appropriate.

Learners as a Resource

Often learners are seen as a drain on the resources of an agency. They require the time of an enabler and others to explain procedures and working practices. Enablers may not be able to take their full allocation of agency work as they have to spend time with the learner and time completing documentation for the university. Learners also need space and access to facilities such as telephones, computers and so on. This argument suggests that the work the learner does is somehow different from the usual work in the agency and probably would not take place if the learner was not present. In fact, the learner generally takes on pieces of work which would need to be completed by other agency members. There is a balance between the learners' drain on agency resources and their addition to agency resources. Sometimes this ends up as a net loss, and at other times it will end up as a net gain. The balance will depend on the capability and stage of the learner, and the level of difficulty of the work within the agency. With the social work degree there is evidence that students can learn by providing and developing services. Doel (2005) reports on one such project set up in response to the unmet needs of refugees. Students were allocated work through a social services referral co-ordinator who provided work-based supervision. All the students had access to a practice teacher. The work was home-based and the organisation referred to as 'virtual'. After two years the project grew, successfully bid for mainstream funding, became a registered charity and now has permanent staff. The direct work with refugees and their families would not have been undertaken without the students. Although significant social work was needed it did not fall within the criteria for intervention by social services. In addition to the individual work with the refugees and their families the students were involved in working with other agencies to integrate services. They also identified barriers within existing agency practices and set about dismantling them. This idea challenges the view that students are a net drain on an agency. This notion can be adapted and used within existing agencies. It is interesting to note that this was common practice for Certificate in Social Service (CSS) students – a sister qualification to the Certificate of Qualification in Social Work (CQSW) for residential and day care service staff.

Learners can be used to identify unmet need within an agency and develop a service to meet that need. Or they could be used to investigate a problem and devise a strategy to overcome it. Think about what learners might do in their placement setting, and perhaps the following examples might stimulate ideas.

- Researching and developing a user friendly pack for young people on admission to a residential unit.
- Investigating ways of organising the decor and layout of a residential unit for older people to help residents with dementia find their way around.

- Making links into the community for residents with learning disabilities.
- Identifying the needs of older ethnic minority group members in relation to meals on wheels and sourcing alternative meals from the local 'take away' shops.

Learners have set up similar projects across the country and they are often taken over as part of mainstream agency provision. As Doel (2005) discovered, learners felt that they could have a real impact on people's lives. With the refugee model the learners had no existing procedures to follow, and they found that starting from where the service user is was quite liberating. In other examples, learners might have to work within existing procedures or make a case for changing them and can experience frustration and resistance whilst demonstrating their skills in working round the obstacles. Not all learners would be suitable for these types of opportunity. The refugee model, for example, found that students who were enthusiastic and motivated fared best. These characteristics were better predictors of success than experience and existing skill base. All those who are engaged in this type of learning will need the support of an enabler who can help them put their learning into a wider context and make sense of it. With proper support learners could provide completely new services or new ways of working within existing services. It is essential that all people who are involved in these sorts of learning arrangements are clear about the roles they play in relation to the learner.

Models of Practice Learning

From the literature (Evans, 1999; Shardlow and Doel, 1996; Thompson, Osada and Anderson, 1990) there seems to be a number of functions which people must perform in order for a learner to learn in practice. These include the following:

- Creating a climate within the work base to learning.
- Developing a relationship with the learner which will encourage them to think critically about practice, reflect on their practice and feel safe to make mistakes, admit their ignorance and try out new ideas.

- Identifying how each individual learner learns best and utilising this information to plan a practice curriculum.
- Specifying learning outcomes for the learner.
- Formulating a plan to enable the learner to meet their learning outcomes.
- Providing teaching/learning opportunities in order to assist the learner meet their learning outcomes.
- Making an assessment plan with the learner which takes place over time and includes measurement against.
- Supervising the learner's practice in order to ensure that they are working to agency and professional standards.
- Providing evidence to the validating body the learner has or has not satisfied their criteria.
- Supporting the learner to overcome any factors which are impeding their progress.
- Negotiating with others for resources and facilities, which may assist the learner to develop.
- Assisting the learner to integrate theory and knowledge into their practice.

Typically, within qualifying programmes, these functions are undertaken by one or two people. If it is one person, they are usually based in the same workplace as the learner and known as the 'on-site practice teacher'. If two people are involved there would usually be one person in the same workplace as the student taking responsibility for the learner's day-to-day practice, referred to as the 'on site supervisor'. The other person would be an 'off site practice teacher' who had links with both the learner and the on site supervisor – and a wider managerial, teaching and assessment role (Lawson, 1998). Central Council for Education and Training in Social Work (CCETSW) (1996) when giving guidance on what they then called the 'long arm' model of practice teaching identified which functions this person should undertake. They stated that the practice teacher should have overall responsibility for the management of the learner's placement and linkage with the programme of study. The practice teacher should also have responsibility for ensuring that direct observation of the student's practice takes place, writing the student's placement report and where necessary attending the examination board. The on-site supervisor should oversee the day-to-day management of the learner's work and identify suitable work for them to undertake in consultation with the practice teacher. The practice teacher is responsible for the integration of theory and practice, developing anti-discriminatory practice and drawing out the values of social work. Both practice teacher and supervisor have responsibility for teaching and assessment.

However, whilst the 'typical' scenario outlined above holds good in many settings, new structures perhaps need to emerge to respond to developments in the field. Social work provision is now more fragmented than previously with the split between the purchaser and provider sectors. Social workers operate in a number of different types of agencies, including the private and voluntary sector, where there may be staff from other professions and staff who may be very experienced practitioners but have no professional qualifications. Their knowledge and expertise should be included in any programme for a social work learner.

Many staff within agencies are interested in helping learners develop but may not be able or willing to undertake all the functions required to enable them in practice. However some staff would like to specialise as enablers of learning, working with several learners at a time. It is not unusual to encounter people who are working as mentors with newly qualified social workers, acting as a practice teacher to a learner on a social work degree programme and acting as an assessor for candidates on National Vocational Qualifications (NVQ) and/or PQ courses. All these factors make it more difficult to locate the functions of the enabler within one or two people. The functions may need to be spread across many different people to create a *learning network*. If all the people involved in the learning network are clear about their roles and all work together then this will bring a richness and depth to the learner's experience. If roles are unclear and the process unmanaged then there is the chance that things will get missed or learners will receive mixed and confusing messages. It requires one person to be the manager of the learning network and the learning process. This person should be responsible for co-ordination of all others involved and could act as a mediator should the need arise.

All the above may sound extremely complicated and unwieldy so putting it into a diagram may help the more visual learner identify how a network might form. The titles of the people involved, for example, practice teacher, mentor, on-site supervisor, and so on, are probably not as important as knowing which person is going to undertake which function.

ACTIVITY

Identifying the roles in learning

Considering the 13 functions identified above, think about a learner in your workbase and the people who might be involved in their learning process. Identify who might undertake what functions in the tables (see two different examples below). It might be that one or two people undertake all the functions and so the process should be relatively easily managed. If they are spread across several people a plan will need to be drawn to manage the network and ensure effective communication between all parties including the learner.

Function	Name	Name	Name	Name
Assisting the learner to integrate theory and knowledge into practice				
Supporting the learner				
And so on				

OR

Name	Name	Name	Name
Support learner	Provide learning opportunities	And so on	And so on
And so on			

A learning agreement would be a good place to identify roles/functions and methods of managing the network.

ACTIVITY

As a way of helping you use the ideas in this chapter and link them to your own situation access a copy of Guidance for Assessing Learning in the Workplace (GSCC/TOPSS 2002) from www.gscc.org.uk and complete the exercise below.

Consider your own learning needs in relation to becoming an enabler.

Look at some of the requirements in Guidance for Learning in Workplace

Identify which knowledge and skills you have already got.

From this identify what your learning needs are.

Can you write these in terms of learning objectives? You could use the guidance document here again to help you.

Identify learning opportunities that will help you demonstrate your learning outcomes.

Identify a person/persons who would be willing to help you.

Formulate an assessment plan for you to be able to demonstrate your competence.

Put your plans into action reviewing progress with your enabler.

Key Learning Points

- Just providing work for the learner with service users and carers does not ensure that they will learn from it.
- Using the NOS for social work or personalised learning outcomes will allow the enabler to plan what work is required.
- Learning opportunities may need to be created to meet learners' needs if they are not available in the work base. These could be available in other parts of the host agency or in other agencies.
- The identification of clear roles for all those involved in the learning process is essential.

CHAPTER 5

Supervision

Theories and Definitions

Ask social workers what sequence of lectures, tutorials or seminars they recollect from their qualifying training and you may struggle to get more than vague memories. Ask them about their placements and their practice teacher and you can usually be offered an impressively detailed reminiscence. If the placement is remembered as the main body of professional learning, then supervision is the beating heart of the placement process – a place where the essence of the placement is distilled, mulled over and savoured for its learning; a place where those fundamental discussions about learning and the critical evaluation of performance are played out. The relatively intense nature of supervision between learner and enabler is another powerful factor in its appeal, as it often sharply contrasts with many qualified workers' experience of supervision as an employee. In turn, our experience of supervision in qualifying training sets a tone and expectation of supervision that seems to follow us through our professional careers. Social workers often seek to re-create good experiences of such supervision in their relationships with learners and enablers – even line managers. Clearly this might not always be appropriate for the simple reason that not all supervision is, or should be, the same. Our starting point here is that whatever supervision is, it is vital for all those involved to create a shared understanding of the nature of their particular supervisory relationship. This chapter will explore some of the dynamics of supervision, unpicking aspects of its nature, processes and problems in an attempt to construct some notions of good supervisory practice.

The complexity of supervision begins to be revealed as we consider its component parts. Kadushin (1976) talks of three functions of social work supervision

- Educative
- Supportive
- Administrative/Managerial.

Within this framework we can detect the role of the enabler as that of 'teacher', 'supporter' and 'assessor' and, in turn, imagine these functions expressed as the three corners of an equilateral triangle – equally import-ant aspects of the supervisory relationship. Of course, the language of the social work degree (GSCC, 2003) deliberately uses the phrase 'prac-tice assessor', seemingly placing an emphasis on the assessment side of this triangle of roles. Indeed, it needs to be acknowledged that the har-mony of an equilateral triangle can often disguise the conflicts inherent within the supervisory process. For example, an enabler who is assessing a failing learner will find himself or herself compromised in providing a certain level of support. Similarly, a learner who expects the supervisory relationship to be one primarily of support may struggle to hear mes-sages of the need to improve or develop practice in certain areas. Some learner/enabler relationships don't possess any aspect of the assessment function; mentor roles can simply exist to advise on the production of a portfolio. What matters is the clarity between the parties of each others' role. To achieve that clarity one needs to explore its nature more deeply.

Thompson, Osada and Anderson (1994) draw on a range of literature to outline what they see as the key principles of supervision:

1. Supervision ensures that client and agency needs are being met. As practitioners, learners have to be accountable to both.
2. Supervision assesses and evaluates learners' learning needs and their ability to practice.
3. Supervision informs the learner's practice.

This typography is helpful for the aspects of supervision that it reveals. The importance of accountability to service user and agency are emphasised and we also see the relegation of the support function which, given the rising concern around accountability within the prac-tice of social care, may be appropriate. We are offered factors of learn-ing and evaluation – which suggest elements of reflection on practice and also of an enabling dialogue. The construction of supervision remains complex although the core ideas, as we have seen from these typologies, are similar.

None of these models takes into account the impact of experience: the nature of both learner's and enabler's experience of supervision. It is sometimes said that the Queen thinks the world smells of fresh paint – as everywhere she goes people will prepare for her arrival. Extending this analogy, if one's only experiences of supervision have been task-orientated, infrequent and harsh then anything different (such as an expectation of reflection) can be quite challenging. It is only by examining (and valuing) this previous experience that either party can adequately understand the constructs already formed within either party's minds regarding the nature, function and process of supervision. For example, as the social work degree brings younger students onto placement, their primary (if any) experience of supervision is perhaps more likely to have been within commercial, private sector settings – but this is not necessarily an inferior experience. Enablers should consider the concept of a 'relational' model of supervision: 'Rather than viewing the student as developmentally immature, or as a novice who is there only to learn from their supervisor's knowledge and expertise, both student and supervisor contribute their insights and utilize the supervisory relationship to further mutual learning and growth' (Ringel, 2001, p. 172).

Similarly, in the process of post-qualifying (PQ) mentorship both parties can have had very different experiences of supervision, both through their qualifying training and beyond into supervision through line management structures and other aspects of their continuing professional development. A relational model allows a process of reflection on experience and the creation of a shared understanding based on the best aspects of supervision encountered and those desired.

As our picture of supervision becomes clearer it feels as though we are able to construct our own definition of supervision as' *A reasoned reflection, An engaging discussion, An illuminating evaluation.'*

Within this definition we see the core premise of a triangle again reflected but with helpful descriptors: reflection is at the heart of this – but within a *reasoned* approach, not purely descriptive but analytical and drawing on experience and knowledge, including notions of evidence bases for intervention, for example. The discussion of work within the supervisory relationship should be *engaging* for both learner and enabler, drawing on the knowledge and experience of both parties but within as equal a dialogue as is consistent with the real differences in power. Finally, the process of assessment is a key element of supervision, especially for the student learner and practice teacher roles. However, if we reflect on the broader issue of the evaluation of practice we can see how this includes, but moves beyond, assessment into the hidden corners of casework, organisational behaviour and teamwork. Supervision needs to bring a light to all these areas and not be purely bound to competence assessment. It needs to assist in the broader evaluation of practice by developing practitioner-researchers. The enabler needs to work to ensure that supervision is *illuminating* – not simply a statement 'how it is' – but with ambitions to reveal or suggest connections, links, causalities and conclusions. It needs to develop sensitivity to the patterns of experience and to the skills we need to develop in order to evaluate practice. As Raelin (2002, p. 66) says of reflective practice, it 'illuminates what the self and others have experienced'. Fundamentally, we have developed the Kadushin triangle (of teaching, support and assessment) to include the necessary reality of its dynamic, expressive and critical nature (discussion, reflection and evaluation) as shown in Diagram 5.1.

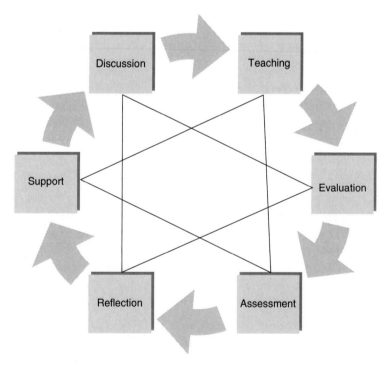

Diagram 5.1 Supervision hexagram

Supervision Changing over Time

How should we construct an understating of supervision beyond, as we have just considered, its component parts and the dialogue between them? Gardiner (1989) is a good place to start as he allows us to enhance our understanding of the fluid process of supervision – its dynamism – that we have tried to capture in the preceding section, but with an awareness that learner and enabler may be at different 'places' at different times. Gardiner, drawing heavily on adult learning research, attempts to develop an interactive model of teaching and learning in supervision. He envisages three levels of interaction but, most importantly, reflects on the tensions of learner and enabler being at *different* levels:

> Level 1 – a focus on the *content* of learning
> 'associated with an expectation that there is a single right way to practise, and that there is a single right way to teach and learn'. (Gardiner, 1989, p. 130)

There is also a hierarchical relationship between enabler and learner.

> Level 2 – a focus on the *process* of learning
> Here enablers see contributions from learners as being vital to the learning process. The process of learning has its own life and is valued. Learners are enabled to have an active role in constructing meaning from their own experiences – the process allows diversity in teaching, learning and practice.

> Level 3 – Meta-Learning and the demonstration of versatility
> Here we see the 'completion' of the dynamic process of supervision where it is recognised that learners will learn in different ways, people can teach in different ways, workers can practise in different ways. We can see the need for different approaches to different tasks, valuing versatility of intervention in accordance with clients presenting issues. (Gardiner, 1989, p. 133)

Gardiner is useful as he illuminates two points: first that both the learner and enabler have different but complementary roles and responsibilities in creating a shared and appropriate delivery of supervision.

The second is that it is equally possible that the practice teacher and student, and mentor and mentee, can be at different places for different reasons at different times. Here, Gardiner provides us with a simple model for exploring that. Consider these simplified examples: The enabler who focuses too much on issues of accountability and the delivery of techniques to intervene. Supervision can struggle in this scenario to rise above 'this is what to do next with Mr Jones'. Similarly, inexperienced learners, less sure of himself or herself in the agency setting (or CPD process), may simply want supervision to be about being told what to do – 'tell me what to do with Mr Jones'. Experienced learners may feel uncomfortable when looking to their mentors – 'I do what I have always done with Mr Jones, is it wrong?' Gardiner seeks a supervisory relationship that has considered, 'what *could* we do with Mr Jones?' In any event, each party should reflect on the developing nature of their supervisory relationship and ask themselves – what kind of supervision are we creating? Thus, we can ask – How can I evaluate my contribution to the supervisory relationship? It would be perfectly appropriate for a beginning learner to be relatively dependent on an enabler at the outset of the learning process – but clearly they would need to move forward as they develop their knowledge, skills and values. This is a complex question to which we shall return, but taking a step at a time, let us consider some preparatory issues connected to supervision.

Roles and Responsibilities

How does the enabler prepare his or her team for the arrival of a learner or, in the case of some PQ mentoring arrangements, how might the learner prepare his or her team for the arrival of an enabler? Of course, these are all elements of supervision planning in one sense. If we take us given the common concept of placements/ learning being with teams rather than individual enablers, it is important to identify issues regarding the role of the enabler alongside other roles in the organisation: team leaders, line managers, colleagues and related colleagues in multi-professional teams. Do all these people need to know how supervision will work and how, if they have feedback, it should be given? A common problem for beginning learners is to be given mixed, confusing or contradictory messages from team colleagues. The enabler has a public relations role with regard to the hosting team, encouraging them to engage with the learning process and helping them to understand how to do so appropriately. Other preparation may include the arrangement of administrative support. enablers must also reflect on the support they will be able to access for themselves in this particular role. Of course, the infrastructure that exists to support the learning process can differ wildly amongst the range of agencies across the statutory, private, voluntary and independent sectors of the broad social care field. Inevitably these differences present not only their own challenges, but also opportunities. Barron notes the arrival of the social care placement for social work students and the complications this can raise for the learner who has particular stereotypical views about the social work role and its presence or parallel in the social care sector – characterised as the 'poor relation'. Of course, with the use of off-site practice teachers, this factor can also extend to enablers (Barron, 2004). It becomes vital to ensure that roles are clear in such settings and the general management of such placements is at a premium. Having said that, the opportunities are often considerable:

> social care placements offer students the opportunity to learn some of the basics of social work practice vis-à-vis communication skills and social work values through their involvement in personal care tasks. The student can move on from here to tackle more complex tasks more clearly perceived to be 'social work' tasks … students can benefit from the considerable experience of a range of staff in such settings (and) … can learn to be more 'self directing'. (Barron, 2004, p. 35)

It would be remiss to continue this section without reflecting on how learners should prepare for supervision. Within the social work degree there is a welcome, much firmer, emphasis on preparation for placement in general – and supervision in particular. Students must take advantage of these learning opportunities; consider their experience of supervision and to begin to imagine the expectations of them in the placement and supervision. Of course, there are the practical aspects of learning about settings and typical interventions, but as we think broadly about this issue, learners should work hard to develop a sense of themselves as an adult learner in this vital element of their professional training.

ACTIVITY

To develop a shared understanding of supervision

First meeting of learner and enabler/first supervision session/informal meeting prior to placement

- Describe your main experience/s of supervision?
- What worked well for you (if anything) about this form of supervision?
- What was difficult, inhibitive or unhelpful?
- If you have not had supervision before, what do you imagine it to be like?
- How do you envisage this supervisory relationship?

  Learners and enablers can separately prepare a list of the following:

- What are the elements of good and bad supervision?
- Compare lists.
- Construct a shared list of good and bad elements of supervision.

Early discussion of these issues allows the development of a shared understanding of supervision. This has to be seen as good practice, particularly around issues of anti-oppressive practice as the two parties establish the premise of supervision, sharing experience and selecting good aspects from that experience to begin positively. Naturally, this active discussion also reveals the *dynamic* aspect of supervision. Supervision of learners is arguably one of the most professionally stimulating opportunities afforded to the social worker. The reason is that supervision possesses these dynamic, unpredictable elements that challenge and provoke.

Preparing for Supervision

Let's imagine a typical set of questions that learners and enablers might ask themselves prior to their supervision session – some will obviously be more appropriate to beginning learners:

Learner

- Have I done what I set out to do at the last session?
- Do I have a clear idea about where my work is going?

- What have I done since the last session that I am pleased about? How has my work improved? What factors have helped me work better?
- What I have done since the last session that I am unhappy about, why did I do it that way? What would help me do it differently in future?
- Is there anything or anyone at work creating a problem for me?
- Have I produced any evidence regarding the competency framework?
- What reading am I familiar with that fits into my work?
- What issues have I dealt with this week that relate to issues of power and oppression – both in my work as part of the team, an organisation and a profession and my work with service users?

Enabler

- Has the learner done what was agreed at the last session?
- Am I satisfied with the quantity and quality of the work?
- What has the learner done since the last session that I am particularly pleased about? How has their work improved? What factors might have helped them work even better? How can I help the learner build on this success?
- What has the learner done since the last session that I am unhappy about? Why did it happen? What could I or other people in the organisation have done to prevent it or make it better? What can we do to prevent such things happening in the future?
- What do I think learners should be concentrating on before the next session? How will this fit into their priorities?
- Do learners seem to be overworking or under-working? Are there problems about timekeeping? Is the learner keeping up with essential administration maintenance and other routine tasks?

Behind Closed Doors

How can I evaluate my contribution to the supervisory relationship and is it appropriate? This personal question – perhaps seldom asked– reminds us that the interior world of supervision is often a closed world, a secret garden. Arguably, the supervision between practice teacher and student is one of the most intensive that most professional careers will contain. Ironically, it is also a relatively unexplored territory and certainly a mystery to those who are embarking on it from an inexperienced background. The next section aims to talk through some of the common elements of supervision – what takes place within the secret garden, sharing some notions of good practice within them.

Case discussion

Case discussion is the building block of the supervisory relationship. Where learners are beginning practice, the emphasis within supervision has to be upon the knowledge needed to do the job. Enablers must be sensitive to levels of previous experience and previous learning. Where learners (and enablers) are more experienced the case discussion can develop into critical discussion perhaps exploring the theoretical and evidence basis for interventions, evaluating practice, critiquing agency policy and structures, and exploring the 'what ifs' of the case in hand (what if this service user was black, white, posed greater risks etc.). Learners need to make connections between their professional experiences and learn not to always see cases as individual instances.

Case study

The case study is an excellent way to capitalise on the expertise of the enabler within the workplace. Construct a scenario, perhaps based on an actual case and use discussion of this as a basis for learning in supervision. What do we recognise when we look at this situation? What are the key features of it? What policies and procedures may be relevant? What are our options for intervention? Particularly for the less experienced learner, case study work offers an opportunity for 'dry runs' within the relative safety of the supervisory relationship. With more experienced parties, case study work can offer less personal case analysis in preparation for example, submission of practice-based assignments.

Observation

Surprisingly, there is no requirement to observe a social work student within the qualifying degree. However, practice in many areas retains a notion of a minimum of three direct observations. Of course, in most settings, because the learner is actually informally observed most of the time, the function of these formal observations needs to be understood differently, that is, the ability to perform professionally whilst being observed. Direct observations are an excellent opportunity for service user involvement in the assessment process of the learner. Great care needs to be taken with the setting up of these observations: consent, confidentiality and feedback to both learner and service user must all be paid close attention, but the benefits are considerable, including offering, 'a good means of modelling inclusive practice' (Edwards, 2003, p. 344).

Learning

Through the process of case discussion, feedback, observation and so forth, the enabler provides learning. There will also be many opportunities for more didactic aspects of teaching. Enablers, especially with beginning learners will be required to teach the basics of the role and need to reflect on what learners need to know and in what order. Enablers need to do this in cognisance of the transferable skills and knowledge already possessed by the learner and in a way that suits their learning style.

Group learning

A common process in many settings, where there is more than one learner on placement at a given time, is group supervision. This can involve all the above exercises worked on with others or perhaps more potently – group discussions. Such discussion can pursue reflective processes and can benefit from a more impromptu and improvisational nature – hence its likening to 'jazz' (Longenecker, 2002). Whilst little research has been conducted into this type of learning, what there is suggests that learners and enablers both feel very positively about its use in social work settings (Lindsey, 2005).

Constructing Supervision

Talking of jazz, the low premium placed upon imagination and creativity in most social care/work settings tends to inhibit the enabler's

ability to construct exercises for supervision. This section simply
aims to provide four broad examples of activities that can help the
learning environment of supervision become stimulating and enjoy-
able. It is noted that research suggests enablers sometimes find it
difficult to provide learning around 'difference' (Maidment and
Cooper, 2002). These exercises, whilst not directly related to power,
can all be focused on a variety of themes including anti-oppressive
practice.

Theory into practice

The whole arena of exploring the relationship between theory and
practice clearly causes some problems for learners and enablers alike.
Schön's (1983) notions of the 'high hard ground' of theory and the
'swampy lowland' of practice are particularly helpful when beginning
to think about this. Most programmes of learning in social work place
an emphasis on 'theory into practice'. We would argue that the core
reason behind this is the importance of fully understanding why we are
doing what we do with our service users. As practitioners and learners
battle within the swamp, it is hard to see beyond the mists of a workload and there is a danger we become 'doer's, rather than 'thinkers'.
We must develop working styles that include an ability to reflect on
what it is from the high ground that helps construct an understanding
of this intervention, this professional dilemma this organisational policy. Without this processes we become narrow, routine and uncritical.
Kolb, a major theorist in this area, argues forcefully that our learning
must be tested out in new situations. Without this process practitioners
may get things right, but not know why. If this is the case, then how can
this learning be taken into new situations? (Kolb, 1983). If we keep a
practical approach to the matter, there are some appropriate activities
that we can employ to assist and these are covered in some detail in the
chapter on reflective practice. We would argue that there is a connection between the impact of our own personal experience, values and
culture, and our professional activity as learners. Using such activities
may also raise awareness of how theory and practice are intertwined,
whilst surfacing the often unspoken knowledge of one's own personal
and family history in relation to practice scenarios. For example, see
the Activity Box.

ACTIVITY

To conduct a personal review

Imagine you are planning to interview the following people (these can be adapted according to the setting)

1. An elderly person who is reluctantly considering admission to a residential home.
2. A young man aged 16 who is to appear in court on a charge of demanding money with menaces from boys in the neighbourhood.
3. A man who has a recurrence of a depressive illness.
4. A woman who reports an incidence of domestic violence.

• Write a paragraph of notes on two of the situations in your list.

Make a list of the different topics that might be the focus of a personal and cultural review of yourself, an enquiry into what your experiences (direct and indirect) have been in relation to the issues raised in these interviews. For example, in relation to the first scenario – who have I cared for? How would I feel about being cared for by a relative? How do I use my free time? How do I react when I cannot do what I want? What balance do I like to draw between my time and time with my family?

Source: adapted from Shaw (1997, p. 39).

Thus, in the activity above a feeling about being cared for by a relative may contain resentment that a learner might become dependent. Their experience of caring may have led them to an awareness of how women can be forced into stereotypical caring roles by male family members and that might be a source of sensitivity to discrimination in society generally and caring roles in particular. In this way learners and enablers can begin to unravel not only the connection between theory and practice, but also between theory, practice and experience. It is often helpful to begin with what the learner (beginning or experienced) knows best – their own experiences: 'Educators helped students understand "difference" by drawing on learning from student's previous life experiences. They also use self disclosure and questioning skills to develop student's awareness, challenge assumptions, and highlight stereotypical thinking' (Maidment and Cooper, 2002, p. 406).

Critical incident analysis

Following Fook's ideas of this process, learners can be asked to focus on (and deconstruct) a critical incident, that is, 'any happening which was significant to a person' (Fook, 2002, p. 98), but which carries some importance in the social work process with a client. Indeed, much of the case study material produced for qualifying and PQ social work awards draws on this process and the following headings form the basis of an essay plan for such work. Learners can base their description and analysis on the following headings:

i.   Brief details of the context and background; reasons the incident is critical and a description of the actual incident.
ii. Analysis of the incident – asking the following types of questions:

   • What patterns emerge from the description?
   • How do I see myself in relation to the players?
   • What knowledge and assumptions have I made and from where do they emanate?
   • How might I have interpreted the situation differently?
   • What is my theory of power within this account? (Fook, 2002, p. 100)

Fook's model is enormously helpful and, in its last question regarding power, reminds of the need to retain a focus on issues of power, inequality, oppression and exclusion.

Process recording

A similar but slightly different activity asks learners to explore the *process* of a particular, usually isolated and singular, interaction – often an interview with a service user. Urbanowski and Dwyer (1988) define process recording as 'the written account of the dynamic interaction that occurs during an interview or in other forms of client contact' (p. 53). Process recordings can be employed with a direct observation of the learner's practice and can be a useful opportunity whether the incident is 'critical' or not. This activity also works well with very brief conversations such as a telephone call or a doorstep conversation. The grid, reproduced from Wilson (1980) with minor adaptations is a useful tool for structuring the process recording.

Enabler's comments	Content-dialogue	Gut-level feeling/response	Learner's analysis/assessment
The enabler can make *comments* and give *feedback* right opposite the interaction or feelings/reactions of the learner's records.	Learner uses this space to record *interaction word-for-word* (as far as is pragmatic/possible). This is to include verbal and non-verbal components. Include all others present, communications such as silence, interruptions, and other interactions which may not be part of the planned intervention or interview.	Record how *you* were *feeling* as the dialogue, activity, or interaction was taking place. Be as open and honest as you can. Use this to look at your feelings and not to analyse the client's reactions.	*Analyse* your interventions; *identify* skills you are using; *assess* your work

Role play

This phrase can be guaranteed to draw groans from most learners and often enablers. In its worst incarnations, role play can feel as though it is an unseen exam on a play that you don't understand – in front of an audience. Role play does, however, have its place within the supervisory relationship but needs to be deployed with some sensitivity. Role playing has significant merit for the learner as it incorporates reflection on practice (how do I do this?) with self-reflection (why am I doing this in the way I am?). As learners and enablers work together within the role play, it becomes a collaborative process of engagement in reflection. Because of its generally poor reception, it is suggested that enablers begin with very short, non-threatening role plays that work to strengths of experience within the learner, taking care not to allow the 'play' to develop into areas of technical know-how which a learner may still be learning. Learners should have roles they can easily engage with and role play in scenarios allows for risk-free rehearsal and can be built up through a period of supervision into more complicated scenarios and, most obviously, in rehearsing upcoming potentially difficult service user interviews. Suggestions for introductory brief role plays could include the following:

- Your neighbour is being harassed by local children and you decide to call on him to see if he is Okay.
- You are on your first home visit on placement to see client X, who answers the door. How do you introduce yourself?
- You are discussing racism with a colleague in the tea room and they say that 'the area is over-run with bloody asylum seekers'.
- Client X has phoned up to cancel your appointment and seems to be avoiding you. It is important that you see him. How might the conversation go?

Power and Supervision Games

This section aims to briefly outline some of the issues surrounding the very complex power dynamics that can exist within supervision, the games that can sometimes be played and to suggest some ways forward. Without wishing to overstate the problem, there can be instances of things 'going wrong' in supervision and the potential for the abuse of power by the enabler is significant (Earwaker, 1992; Lee, 1998; Sharp and Danbury, 1999). Supervision has to attend to two aspects of power – as it affects the work of the learner: anti-discriminatory practice (ADP) as it applies to work with service users and, as it affects the power relationship between the learner and the enabler. Enablers have particular responsibilities to ensure that, depending on their role in the learning relationship, they both own the power they have and deploy it appropriately. Thompson's ubiquitous PCS model can be borrowed to initially explore the power dynamics of supervision by focusing on the personal, the cultural and structural (Thompson, 1997).

What differences exist in these regards between the learner and the enabler? What might their impact be if not attended to? Importantly, Thompson reminds us that as we analyse the arena of personal discrimination (and this includes practice), we find it proportionately more amenable to influence than the other levels. Supervision provides an important avenue therefore for the questioning and challenging of our assumptions. The application of an understanding of power to the supervisory relationship can result in the modelling of positive practice elsewhere by the learner. Thus, for example, if the male enabler can demonstrate sensitivity to the needs of the female learner within supervision, she can take learning from that modelling into her practice. Sadly, the reverse will also be true and if enablers display a lack of sensitivity to these issues, then they are effectively teaching discriminatory practice. If you aren't part of the solution then you are part of the problem or, as Hawkins and Shohet put it, we need to learn, 'the humility of being the care taker of the therapeutic space' (2000, p. 10).

The enablers' responsibility to be part of the solution involves reflecting on the obvious differences that exist between the learner and themselves. Think of race, gender, age, disability, class and experience – are these differences present? How might they impact on the supervisory relationship? Phillipson (2002) reminds us that we need to ensure that we approach these issues with an awareness of their complexity and their impact on identity. One might also seek a constructive dialogue between learner and enabler to ensure that discussion about, for example, a learner's identity (and experience) as an experienced black female social worker in a mainly white organisation is centred on the learner's view rather than the assumptions of the enabler. This is not necessarily a complicated area – simply create space in supervision to ask the questions – and don't assume that such matters are static; they are dynamic and change overtime. As Phillipson says, the supervisory process should be engaged with, 'valuing and surfacing uncertainty, ambiguity, plurality and narrative in supervision as well as in practice' (Phillipson, 2002, p. 249). On this note it is interesting to reflect on McHale and Carr's work looking at the issue of gender in 40 different supervisory relationships between family therapists and their trainees in Dublin (McHale and Carr, 1998). Contrary to a stereotypical expectation, female supervisors tended to be more directive and interrupted more often, whilst male supervisors tended to work more collaboratively. Whilst the authors (and ourselves) would not wish to make any great claims for the research, it is included to remind us that one's assumptions may not always be correct. We must retain an open, critical approach to supervision.

Forming a platform for this type of supervision also implies the creation of a certain level of trust. Enablers wishing to create a supportive atmosphere should pay attention to the permission of mistakes, the open expression of concerns, discussion of 'taboo' subjects and being able to share one's own thoughts and feelings as an enabler with the learner (Schulman, 1982). Furthermore, as Cousins reminds us, we cannot expect the learner to simply trust us from the start – these things have to be earned: 'we are kidding ourselves if we pretend that power differences either do not matter or have been overcome' (Cousins, 2004, p. 177).

Of course, as Phillipson (2002) notes, there is something of an orthodoxy within social work that power is oppressive of itself. Enablers and practice teachers in particular, will be acutely aware that the power they hold, especially in its assessment and gate keeping function, has many positive and constructive aspects. Power is a complex issue and it may be that enablers need to transfer some learning from the literature of empowerment, as has been suggested by Clark (2000, p. 29). It is most illuminating to reflect on the work of Gutiérrez, an African-American feminist writing on empowerment of individuals. She argues that practitioners need to be able to pursue five interventions which, when listed seem to correspond with the enabler's role in supervision:

1. accepting the clients definition of the problem
2. identifying and building upon existing strengths
3. engaging in a power analysis of the clients situation
4. teaching specific skills
5. mobilizing resources and advocating for clients. (Gutiérrez, 1990, pp. 151–2)

However, just as some models of empowerment are criticised for focusing on the individual to correct their own situation, rather than the struggle against broader socio-political situations, we must not forget that many models of supervision emphasise support and empowerment as if there were no constraints on the relationship (such as assessment functions) or, indeed, that learners are powerless. Learners can and do exert power within the supervisory process and to conclude this chapter we want to explore some of the complexities of supervisory relationships that can exist around what has been called 'game playing'. Ford and Jones (1987) were one of the first authors to explore this issue within social work supervision, using scenarios that are as valid today as they were then – and give us a useful illustration of the sorts of things that we are seeking to explore.

Example A
The enabler wants to be seen as helpful and offers to be available and supportive all the time. In this scenario the enabler can end up over-identifying with learners, and colluding with them against the agency. Enablers can choose to deny the element of authority in the super-visory relationship, perhaps fearing rejection. The game becomes one of emotional blackmail: 'I'm being nice to you and I expect you to be nice to me' – it's all too cosy for learning to take place.

Example B
This scenario revolves around the learner who says, 'If you give me work, I'll be uncritical and you won't have any problems with me'. Students may be reluctant to be pushed intellectually, but will always look for new work, new situations, and volunteering for work at team meetings – and then excusing themselves as being too busy. The enabler's response is to become more controlling, rationing work and taking responsibility away from the learner. This, in effect, creates dependency in the learner and his or her involvement in the placement decreases. The learner does not take responsibility for his or her own learning, admits ignorance and says, 'what would you do?', 'how should I handle this?' The learner can end up saying, 'I did exactly what you told me and look what happened' (Ford and Jones, 1987, pp. 76–78).

With these two brief examples we see the complexity of the learner – enabler relationship and the many dimensions of power. Whilst it is certainly clear that enablers (especially practice teachers) are relatively powerful in relation to the learner, it would be a mistake to see the equation as fixed (as our examples show). Power dynamics around race, gender, class – the more obviously structural issues can also be combined with other aspects of power relationships that are not always so easily identified within these 'games'.

Raven and French's excellent work on types of power helps further illustrate the problem. As we conclude this chapter let us consider their five forms of power and apply them to the learner–enabler relationship.

Coercive power: *the power to force someone to do something against their will.* Of course this sounds extreme, but perhaps there may be instances where practice teachers ask students to take a particular case on, do a particular duty, report, presentation, direct observation – which is 'naturally' complied with by the relatively powerless student.

Reward Power: *the power to give people what they want and, in return, to get them to do things for you.* Perhaps the enabler exacts some reward for their approval of the learner's practice – a practice teacher can withhold access to cases and resources until they are satisfied that it is appropriate. This can work in the opposite direction: what of the impact of the learner 'rewarding' the enabler ('you're such a great social worker').

Legitimate Power: *the power invested in a role.* Of course, practice teaching is a fabulous example of this. The practice teacher has the power, through their role, to dictate the allocation of work and the assessment of practice. Here, the enabler is the gatekeeper to the profession. Experienced learners as qualified social workers, obviously have greater legitimate power.

Referent Power: *the power from another person wanting to please you or be like you.* Again, this is one that learners and enablers may well relate to. Because of the wealth of legitimate power in the practice teacher role, it is arguably a foolish student that does not contemplate wanting to 'please' the practice teacher. One of the difficult aspects of this is the issue of how far as enablers one is aiming to produce a 'clone' of yourself. How far, as a practice teacher, are you able to applaud the work of your student when it is not done as you would have done it?

Expert Power: *being in possession of knowledge and skills that someone else requires.* What finer description could we have of the power in the enabler role? By definition as an enabler you are in a position of expert in your social work role, so much so that you are expected to share that learning and experience with others for their professional development. This applies strongly to both mentor roles where the intricacies of post-qualifying portfolio compilation allow ample opportunity for expert advice.

Source: French and Raven (1960)

In this chapter we have attempted to draw a picture of supervision; learning that it is a mistake to assume that the image the learner and enabler have of supervision is shared, and enablers must take responsibility in creating that shared understanding in order to avoid confusion and difficulties later on. We have tried to illustrate what goes on in supervision, although, in many ways, this entire book serves a similar purpose as it looks at adult learning, reflective practice and learning partnerships. Whilst we acknowledge the constrictions that surround our learning partnerships and our discussions in supervision, the scope for creative teaching remains enormous and we encourage learners and enablers alike to look imaginatively at supervision and to enjoy it. The development of the degree, PQ training and a range of literature around supervision allows us to articulate and share new ideas. Learners and enablers should use the material offered as a spring board for creative supervision: why ride a bicycle when you could fly?

> Reinventing the wheel is a wasteful and dispiriting activity. Now that we have a language to describe the experience of practice teaching and learning we have an opportunity to spend more time creatively: to extend the metaphor, using the wheels to build different kinds of vehicles for the learning. (Doel, 2000, p. 167)

Key Learning Points

- Different people have different conceptions of what supervision is like. Do not assume anyone else shares your understanding.
- Learners and enabler must prepare for supervision to get the most out of it.
- The experiences of the learner and the enabler are a valuable commodity – use them.
- Be sensitive to the issue of power within supervision – check it out.
- Creative supervision benefits the learner and the enabler.

CHAPTER 6

Reflective Practice

Definitions and Overview

The notion that social work and reflection go hand in hand is both persistent and powerful. Lines can be traced in educational literature on the subject and its application to social work back a number of decades (Dempsey et al., 2001; Gould and Taylor, 1996). Some arenas of learning, such as nursing, are coming to this particular table rather later (Burns and Bulman, 2000) – but a parade of authors have lined up stressing the relevance and importance of the concept and its application in practice for learners. And yet, as Graham Ixer (1999) quite rightly complains, its definition has always been ambiguous as well as contested. Whether one agrees with Ixer's conclusion that there is 'no such thing as reflection' is another matter to which we will return. This chapter aims to draw out some of the key notions in understanding what reflection actually 'is', establishing its relevance to practitioners, learners and enablers and offering some activities and models to facilitate the reflective process.

Our first steps in reflection are perhaps the most important as they help start us off in the right direction. Let us imagine a hot summer's day, a beach holiday and a decision to go for a swim in the sea. How will you go about this? Are you the sort of person who will make a swift choice and run as fast as possible into the chilly waters? Is that the way you always do this, do you like to 'get it over with'? Or perhaps you are more hesitant at the water's edge, letting the water slowly cover your toes, then your ankles and so on (we are grateful to my colleague Alison Ronan for permission to use this illustration). In thinking about these choices – what we might do – we are evaluating our experiences and knowledge to not only think about our action but perhaps to reflect on why we act in a particular way, in particular circumstances and perhaps what that says about us. We are reflecting. We are looking at an aspect of experience, real or imagined, and trying to understand it better by considering and questioning our thoughts. It is important to begin with ourselves as people and to consider the impact of our experiences because, as Schulman notes, 'the capacity to be in touch with the service user's feelings is related to the worker's ability to acknowledge his or her own' (Schulman, 1984, p. 64). Reflection on practice has to be connected with who we are, what we have done and what we might do in the future. Seidel neatly argues that the reflective learner looks backward, inward, outward and forward (Seidel and Blythe, 1996). The concept, as noted above, is not new. John Dewy, writing in 1933 from an educationalist perspective, defined reflection as 'An active, persistent and careful consideration of any belief or supposed form of knowledge in the light of the grounds that support it and the further conclusion to which it tends' (Dewey, 1933, p. 9).

For Dewey, learning was an experiential activity – it was about the continuum of experiences we gather, each influencing the next. So, just as our first swim in the sea would have had a particular quality, subsequent dips are inevitably influenced by that experience in a sort of building-block way. Professional experiences are, of course, very similar and Dewey reminds us that we build professional knowledge and expertise from the very experience of being a social worker. Dewy argues that without reflection our actions become habitual or capricious – both exceedingly worrying characteristics of professional practice. But does Dewey take us quite far enough? Whilst Dewey notes that we must 'actively consider' these experiences there is something akin to a notion that they are all 'bottled up' like wine and savoured at our leisure in a supposedly objective manner. There is a passive notion behind it that ignores the crucial impact of the learner and who they are. David Boud takes this next step in defining reflection as 'A generic term for those intellectual and effective activities in which individuals engage to explore their experiences in order to lead to a new understanding and appreciation' (Boud et al., 1985, p. 19).

Here we see an understanding of the emotive context of experience and Boud offers something new – a sense of an emergent understanding – not just an accumulation of experiences but a deeper, more complex understanding based on those experiences that enables the reflector to contextualise and understand the substance of those experiences at a more profound level. Boud did not see this as a complicated process. Indeed, he elsewhere uses quite prosaic prose to describe reflection as an activity in which people 'recapture their experience, think about it, mull it over, and evaluate it' (Boud et al., 1985, p. 15). Boud helpfully moves us on in developing the concept, but perhaps we can also detect some gaps in his framework, particularly in the professional arena, that is, where do others fit in? How can our professional dialogues be purely internal? How can the development of good quality service delivery result from our reflections upon our experiences? Donald Schön's writings, notably *The Reflective Practitioner: How Professionals Think in Action* (1983) manages to combine these missing elements into a more satisfactory whole. Dewy and Boud had both approached the concept of reflection from a primarily educational perspective whilst Schön's background contrasts with its more philosophy-based approach, combined with his experiences within architecture. In any event, it is interesting to note that none of these thinkers was ever a social worker. However, Schön locates his approach in a context all too familiar within the social work arena, namely the crisis of confidence in the established professional knowledge bases – where the public and policy makers have moved far more, in recent times, to question the way professionals go about their daily activities. Schön questions whether the established bodies of knowledge used by the professions are adequate to deal with the complexity of the social world they ostensibly aim to cater for. Schön makes much of the work arena's complexity, uncertainty, instability and uniqueness. Moreover, he acknowledges the value conflicts that exist for the professional – surely legion in the daily conduct of the social work practitioner. For Schön, there simply *cannot be* a policy, procedure or theory to deal with this unconfinable complexity and because of this, the professional deals in the 'irreducible element of art' (Schön, 1983, p. 18). For Schön, experienced professionals can display artistry in their ability to work in these complex scenarios and, most importantly from our perspective, even though practice is art – it can be taught by enablers and learnt by learners. Schön thought that this artistry spoke to a gap between theory (which could not embrace this complexity) and practice – from which complexity could not be detached: 'In the varied topography of professional practice, there is a high, hard ground where practitioners can make effective use of research-based theory and techniques, and there is a swampy lowland where situations are confusing "messes" incapable of solution' (Schön, 1983, pp. 42–3).

Perhaps many social workers will feel that the analogy of the 'swampy lowland' makes more emotive sense than the 'high hard ground', and Schön, in making these characterisations, helps the professional worker to more fully understand both the limits of technical knowledge – and theory – and the value of experience at the rough end of the worker's day. Ixer complains that Schön bases his research from the point of view of professions (such as architecture) which were less likely to be, 'challenged by the demands of rapid problem solving than social work' (Ixer, 1999, p. 29). But this point fails to challenge Schön's basic premise. For Schön, the swamp – whoever was in it – contained the problems of greatest concern and complexity. Yet this was not some descent into the nihilism of arbitrary action where any one intervention is as good as another and eclecticism reigns. Schön didn't want professionals not to think about what they were doing just because a theory did not "fit". Rather he sought to integrate reflection and understanding with practice. Indeed, Schön was keen to embrace the value of the professional's 'spontaneous, intuitive performance' – which, in its patterns of action, actually demonstrates how much professionals know: 'It seems right to say that our knowing is in our action' (Schön, 1983, p. 49). Schön invites reflective practitioners to question themselves in order to facilitate the process of reflection, although the same can obviously be done in a dialogue between learner and enabler.

ACTIVITY

To explore complex or challenging scenarios in practice

Think of a piece of work in which you are currently engaged and ask yourself these questions:

What procedures am I enacting when I perform this skill?
How am I framing the problem that I am trying to solve?
What features do I notice when I recognise this thing?
What are the criteria by which I make this judgement?

This activity attempts to get us to take a step back from the demands and tensions of the individual case, to try and locate it within wider areas of understanding, to connect it with other areas of our knowledge and experience, and to move beyond simply 'doing'. Schön does not offer a magic bullet to solve our problems, he knows how difficult it can be in the swamp, but he points us in the direction of reflection as a way to value and capitalise on our ideas and experience. For Schön it is the process of reflection in (and on) action that is central to the 'art' by which practitioners deal well with complex situations. Schön's legacy appears extremely relevant to the problems of learning in an uncertain professional world in the following ways:

- *Creative thinkers can best adapt to an uncertain world* – in this context the social worker becomes an artist, a creator of new ways of dealing with difficult, 'messy' situations.
- *'Practicum' (groups of professionals discussing practice) can deal with the log-jams and messiness of practice.* Although not discussed in detail here, this is an important aspect of Schön's connection between reflection and service delivery. In a social work context, Schön might argue that team meetings should focus less on the organisation's needs than on providing a forum where practitioners can share their reflections on professional action. In doing so experiences can be brought together, identified and new ways forward found.
- *Exploring ideas and approaches before and after use.* Again, in the social work context we can conjecture that there is not necessarily a 'right' way of doing things. Schön encourages the professional worker to try out new ways of working to best adapt to changing client need and developing practice knowledge.
- *Organisational structures and defences need to be examined in relation to task.* Another key contribution from Schön is the acknowledgement that reflection takes place within an organisational setting that may or may not develop and adapt (or respond to) client need. Reflective practice must therefore include an examination of existing policy and procedure in relation to service delivery.
- *The context of continuous change as the backdrop to learning.* Schön reminds us that change is an ongoing aspect of professional working life and should be embraced rather than offered as an excuse for inaction or failure to reflect.

Although Schön undoubtedly forms the cornerstone of the literature in the field of reflective practice, one can fairly readily see in which directions one might develop his ideas. Writers such as Friere (1972) take these dynamics and develop the role of enablers in a broader political context, emancipating the learner (and themselves) by challenging the accepted realities of an oppressive world. More recently, Taylor and White have applied a concept of *reflexivity* specifically to the context of social care, taking Schön's ideas a significant step forward: 'Our central argument is that, in the world of health and welfare practice, the pursued ideal of dependable scientific knowledge may well prove elusive and that other approaches which foreground understanding rather than explanation and prediction may more fruitfully be explored' (Taylor and White, 2000, p. 5).

Whilst clearly sharing Schön's views about lack of confidence in the professions and the nature of complexity, Taylor and White take great pains to move forward from the concept of reflection to that of 'reflexivity' which, from their perspective, takes the next step of the idea's development as it directly questions and critiques issues that reflection takes for granted. They argue that the 'bending back' of reflexivity is about the collective action of a professional group subjecting its own knowledge and practice to analysis:

> knowledge is not simply a resource to deploy in practice. It is a topic worthy of scrutiny. We need to question the discourses within which social workers, nurses, doctors and others work, and indeed compare them. How does attachment theory shape our thinking about childhood, children's 'needs' and the role of mothers and fathers? How does biological psychiatry shape our thinking about mental illness and its treatment? We also need to think about how the client/ practitioner relationship and the concept of needs are constituted within (health and welfare) practice. (Taylor and White, 2000, p. 199)

Taylor and White helpfully take us to a more fundamental critique and exploration of the concept of reflection. With them we are invited to question the roots of our knowledge and understanding of our place in the world – our world view – and its relationship to the theoretical and political structures that help shape that view. Kondrat, drawing on this theme talks of 'critical reflectivity' revolving around three questions: first about *the world*; second questions about *my world*; and third questions about *correspondence and contradictions between those worlds* (Kondrat, 1999, p. 465). There are interesting connections to be made here with the epistemological discussions around research methodology. These debates focus on issues such as the nature of truth, knowledge and understanding: particularly important matters for practitioners, researchers, learners and enablers. How do we know what we know? How true is what we take to be true? Perhaps these questions sound fanciful, high hard ground material – but why should not we question, perhaps within supervision, the constructs of social work that inhabit a broad social care discourse? What do we understand by words such as 'independence', 'systems', 'care', 'exclusion', 'risk' and 'power' – where have they come from? What do they mean? Does everyone share a common understanding of them? Which words are more powerful than others?

We could argue that reflexivity simply takes reflection onto more fundamental levels and is not a radical departure from Schön's original principles. Certainly Taylor and White remind us that the 'high hard ground' of theory is as much a contested arena as the debate on what constitutes good practice in a particular setting – these things all bend and move in time in the shifting eddies of such things as politics, knowledge and experience. In one sense we are usefully reminded that we should question our questions.

Reflection, the notion of power and this fundamental challenging of accepted 'reality' are forcefully brought together by the Brazilian writer Paulo Friere who saw the development of critical thought as essential to emancipation and liberation (Friere, 1972). For Friere, education was a liberating force; critical reflection would allow the individuals to appraise, recreate and improve their own reality (Redmond, 2004). According to Friere, learners could become disempowered by what he called the 'banking system' of education – where the teachers are powerful, knowledgeable and dynamic whilst students appear passive, ignorant and accepting. A new style of education had to be developed that broke down these vertical, authoritarian and didactic characteristics. Friere argued for a circular dialogue between learners and enablers where: 'The teacher is no longer merely the-one-who-teaches, but one who is himself taught in dialogue with the students, who in their turn while being taught also teach' (Friere, 1972, p. 53).

In such winning turns of phrase, Friere (1972, p. 54) talks of the need for enablers to 'constantly reform their reflections in the reflection of the (learner)'. Reflection on its own carries little merit and becomes verbal 'blah', whilst action without reflection was action for action's sake. Friere wanted reflection and action to come together in dialogue to 'name the world' (Redmond, 2004). 'Men are not built in silence, but in word, in work, in reflection-action' (Friere, 1972, p. 61). In this essentially reflexive approach, Friere reminds us how the politics of learning influence the supervisory relationship and the nature of critical reflection within that. Mezirow, building on this line of Friere's thought, talks of the importance of transforming the individual's 'meaning perceptions – the structure of assumptions that constitutes a frame of reference for interpreting the meaning of an experience' (Mezirow et al., 1990, p. xvi). For Mezirow, similarly to Friere, the process of transforming an individual's frame of reference beings with critical reflection which, 'addresses the question of the justification for the very premises on which problems are posed or defined in the first place' (Mezirow et al., 1990, p. 12).

Of course, there are problems with these approaches. We are never quite clear with Friere as to the actual process of reflection within his writings. Neither he nor Mezirow adequately deal with how difficult it can be for enablers and learners to change their deep-rooted perspectives on many issues. There are limits, of course, to what an enabler can achieve with any learner, dependent on his or her beliefs, openness to change and, of course, the amount of time the learner and enabler are together. Furthermore, surely enablers may appropriately carry some aspects of the role of 'expert' with beginning learners – they have to be assured that service user's interests are not compromised. But these concerns must not allow us to dismiss Friere's challenge of casting off or casting doubt on all our received wisdoms and knowledge – there is a sense in which the enabler must be reborn: 'an educator is a person who has to live in the deep significance of Easter' (Friere, in Taylor, 1993, p. 53).

Reflexive thinkers such as Taylor and White, and political emancipators such as Friere and Mezirow would both interrogate the very word 'reflection' for its hidden bias, assumptions and political context. Ixer uses an aspect of this line of argument to query our use of reflection at all (Ixer, 1999). He argues that for all the writers on reflection and the different definitions that have been arrived at over the years, no broad agreement has been reached as to what it really means. Ixer argues that this raises far more questions than answers – what is it we are talking about? Do we understand this in the same way? Particularly, he queries, how fair is it to expect learners to be 'reflective' when such a lack of consensus exists about what 'reflective' means? Are enablers actually exerting power in their relationship with learners by requiring them to engage with this process? Of course, Ixer has a point – and we must be sensitive especially to the uses of power and the learner's relative lack of it. However, we can challenge Ixer on a number of counts. Definitions (of reflection) and the differences between them can be overstated in Ixer's relativist world. If we ask ten social workers for a definition of 'social work', then we will likely get as many different answers. This does not mean that each of those people functions without a sufficient degree of shared understanding to enable them to fulfil their complex working duties. Perhaps we can draw an analogy with an elephant – we might all describe it differently, or find it hard to describe – but we would all know if one walked into the office! Second, we should challenge Ixer's concern that students are, in some ways, assessed on their ability to reflect. Learners engaged in programmes of study can be assessed against various competency and standard structures. Asking learners to explain their thinking about why they work in a particular way seems a fair enough way of enabling learning and demonstrating they know what they are doing. And anyway, what is the alternative? Nevertheless, whilst many authors broadly welcome the notion of reflective practice it remains a concept that is both problematic and contentious (Ruch, 2002; Parsloe, 2001). Ixer reminds us that we need to create a shared sense of reflection in our learning relationships and some of the models described later in this chapter can facilitate that process.

Before we do that, it is interesting to pursue a broad critique of the concept of reflective practice through another route: feminism. Clegg (1999) writes convincingly of her view of the epistemology of the concept. She argues that reflective practice is promoted in areas of health and social work where large numbers of women are employed and where levels of autonomy are under attack. Interestingly, she continues, one can view reflective practice as a form of self-surveillance: 'The analysis of reflective practice as disciplinary regime is illuminating since many of the practices of reflection based on diarising, self-monitoring of actions, and interventions, share aspects of the confessional and are monitored through surveillance. Reflective practice understood in this way is a normalizing practice' (Clegg, 1999, p. 172).

Thus, we see another face of reflective practice – a system of surveillance. Notions of competence and compliance can become the yardsticks against which learners are measured – leaving them powerless to effect real change in practice. Reflective practice is thus a politicised concept and our employment of it must include an awareness of its *political* nature. If one chooses to juxtapose the words direct observation (of practice) and surveillance, one can readily see the potential for reflection within supervision taking on this aspect. Both Clegg (1999) and Ruch (2002) make connections between reflective practice and modernity – where science becomes the basis for decisions and progress. Ruch, for example, talks of the danger of using reflective practice to search for an objective truth – where one method of intervention becomes the only way to intervene and performance management methods of organisations assess practitioners to ensure that they are doing things the 'right' way. What gets lost within this analysis is the *emotional* complexity of practice by the very reason that it cannot be quantified (Ruch, 2002; Dominelli, 1996). With all these arguments from the 'high, hard ground', learners and enablers must test their reflection's validity against the realities of the practice in which they operate. Thus, enablers must watch the tendency to produce learners in their own image; they must allow learners their differences and mistakes. But this is not *carte blanche* to operate in ways that are unprofessional. Similarly, whilst learners and enablers may reflect on the politicised notion of competence (Dominelli, 1996; O'Hagan, 1996), perhaps lambasting the reduction of social work to a list contained within the National Occupational Standards, they will still have to be evidenced.

Models of Reflection

We have spent some time assessing the usefulness of the concept of reflection and critically analysing it as a premise. However, for all the debates, there is still a significant expectation of reflection within social work education that commonly exists in our constructs of supervision and portfolio construction. Trying to incorporate some of the ideas we have considered, there are a number of practical activities that we have already begun to touch on in the chapter on supervision that the enabler can utilise to engage the learner in the process of reflection – but first we need to think about the learning environment in which our learner will reflect. A beginning learner's arrival on his or her first placement is often a particularly memorable experience for many reasons. Enablers reflecting back (either as a memory of personal learning or as someone awaiting the arrival of a new learner), would do well to recall some of the feelings the situation evoked. The extent to which learners develop is highly dependent on the prompts and opportunities for reflection provided by the enabler. Clearly, the more comfortable learners feel about discussing their professional behaviour, the more likely the positive learning will accrue. It has been argued that the climate for learning is 'critical' and reliant upon an 'atmosphere of safety' (Dempsey et al., 2001). Do the learner and enabler agree on when we think best?

Diagram 6.1 Reflection

Diagram 6.1 reminds us that reflection, whilst thought of as a cerebral activity is, of course, rooted in the real world. The environment that enablers create for the learner – whether this is in a team, an office or simply within the confines of supervision – is very important. If one wants to get the most out of the reflective process then we need to pay attention to the environment for learning. Indeed, it can become a constructive exercise to think about one's own learning environment – to step outside the daily activities which surround our professional practice. What would someone see if they viewed this setting with dispassionate eyes, free from all the connections, memories, politics and dynamics with which one can become so familiar that they cease to be noticeable?

If we stay rooted in the real world then the learner and enabler will meet in the forum of the supervisory relationship. Here we offer some simple tools to facilitate the process of reflection. This is often done in a questioning model – just like the questions from Schön earlier. Try out these models in supervision, or in a learning log to see which helps the learner or enabler to gain a deeper understanding of a particular professional experience. These models are also invaluable aide-memoirs for writing about practice as they offer, in effect, an outline plan of case (incident) analysis.

Reflective questioning is a good place to begin the process of making *explicit* the *implicit* thinking we have generated. The first model is straightforward and excellent for beginning learners who are new to reflection or are perhaps struggling to develop the reflective habit. This model might also assist experienced practitioner learners who, perhaps so used to doing (rather than thinking, or even less so explaining) that reflection feels strange, even threatening. The model, by Brockbank and McGill is a useful list of open questions designed to engage the learner with their first steps of thinking about practice – focusing on a 5WH model: who, what, where, when and how? Enablers and learners can begin to interrogate experiences with this model. It is important in approaching practice with this model to focus on the key issues and to identify the specific actions that need to be taken in any given situation. Here are two illustrations of how the '5WHs' can be used (Diagram 6.2).

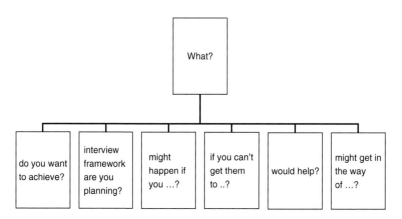

Diagram 6.2 The 5WH model: what?

As these questions move into the midst of intervention and its evaluation, their tenor might change: what were you trying to achieve? What affected the interview/meeting? What do you think was happening when? What changes would you make in the future? What did you do differently this time? (Diagram 6.3).

These types of questions perhaps constitute the gentler nursery slopes of reflection – they can be used as questions for enablers to ask learners – for learners to ask themselves. They prompt us to break out of tendencies within learning relationships to focus on the technical and the procedural. It could be argued that reflective questioning like this sits outside the pragmatic knowledge requirements of learning in a professional setting. There will often be legislation that directs intervention, a proforma that circumscribes some aspects of assessment – learners must get to grips with these issues alongside their reflections upon practice. However, if we take to heart Schön's notion of artistry in professional practice, we can see that Brockbank and McGill do not deny the important emotional context of reflection. Jan Fook, in *The Reflective Researcher* (1996) develops a model that, whilst similar, develops these streams of thought, goes deeper and becomes more reflexive (Diagram 6.4). She codifies the approach as: *Identify, Reflect and Develop.*

Fook's impressive model takes us deep into the reflexive territory lacking in many models. Fook argues for the importance of evolving

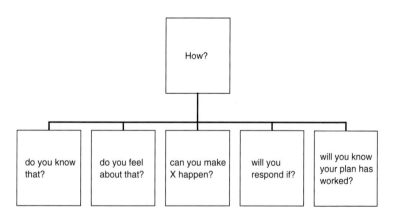

Diagram 6.3   The 5WH model: how?

Source: Adapted from Brockbank and McGill (1998).

> Identify and describe the practice/experience and its context.
> Be as concrete and specific as possible. Context should include issues which are important e.g. organisational issues, professional issues, time of day or week, other people involved.

> Reflect on the account.
> What themes emerge? How are thoughts, feelings and interpretations connected? What interpretations did I make and whose interpretations are they? How did my interpretations influence the situation? How might the situation have been interpreted differently by someone else from a different perspective? What assumptions are implied in my account? Where do these assumptions come from? Are they mine? Where are the gaps and biases in my account?

> Develop
> How does what happened compare with what I thought would happen? Was the theory I thought I was acting upon different from what is implied by my actions? What is similar or different about this experience compared with other experiences I have had? How does my practice need to be changed as a result of this experience?

Diagram 6.4   Identity, reflect and develop

and emergent themes (reminiscent of Schön's: what features do I notice when I recognise this thing?). She also takes us more firmly into the arena of interpretation and meaning, and challenging the assumed 'gaps and biases' in our accounts. Importantly, Fook provides a platform for the critical appreciation of the theoretical nature of the approach. In turn, we can see that this again takes us back to Schön, who argues strongly that it is not sufficient to simply have an experience of something to learn about it. Without reflecting upon the intervention, the team meeting and the supervision session, the experience may be lost or misunderstood. He believes that through this process of reflection we can generate broader understanding, generalisations and new concepts from which we can then be better equipped to tackle new situations and make connections between theory and practice because, after all, it is little use getting it right without knowing why (Schön, 1983).

Theory into Practice

The evidencing of theory into practice is one of the necessary hurdles of learning and teaching in social work. Learners often struggle to grapple with it – concerned at its meaning. Enablers wrestle with their creativity for illuminating learning opportunities and (perhaps secretly) are often also concerned with its meaning. Of course, reflection has to be an integral part of understanding the relationship between what we do and how we understand what we do. This is not a 'one-off' portfolio notion either; reflection is an ongoing process that needs to be an integral part of everyone's professional practice. This section, whilst still dealing with reflective practice, focuses specifically on techniques to encourage reflection on the link between theory and practice. Enablers will find that learners can be at many different stages of familiarity with theory and will have to adapt to their learner's needs. Authors such as Dempsey, Halton and Murphy (2001) talk of 'scaffolding' the process of reflective learning, by which they mean the construction of a sequence of learning opportunities to build the skills of reflection. Similarly, these practical activities can be used to develop an awareness of where the theory of the 'high, hard ground' assists in the reflection on practice in the 'swampy lowland'. Theory is, of course, a broad concept in itself and, at its heart, a theory is simply an *explanation*; a set of statements used to explain or predict a phenomenon. Learners and enablers tend to be particularly interested in theories *of social work practice and method* (such as crisis intervention, task-centred work, solution focused intervention and so forth) and theories that *contribute to* social work (such as sociological and psychological theories that concern, for example, the family, child development, adolescence, offending and behaviour). However, as Payne points out, there are also theories *about* social work which concern the nature of social work in society and theories *of* social work which are concerned with the activities and ambitions of social work. Let's take a practical step forward and think, in particular, of seven different activities we can use to stimulate the connection between theory and practice.

Use a newspaper cutting

One of the benefits of working within the social care arena is that it is rarely out of the news. Considering a newspaper article that relates to the work environment enables the learner to disassociate reflection with academic critique – which, in many cases, the very process of assessment in social work education consistently underlines. Learners can read the article and pick out key aspects of the story, then think how we can understand the message of the piece and, more importantly, the ideas that underpin the message – where do they come from? What might the impact be if those ideas were promoted in this work setting?

Consider the same case from different theoretical perspectives

Select a case from the learner's or enabler's caseload, one that both parties are fairly familiar with. Each person can take one approach – counselling, cognitive behavioural approaches, empowerment, crisis intervention and so forth – and apply that approach to the individual case. Having prepared some material each can briefly present his or her understanding of the approach and how it would apply to the case. Reflection can then take place about issues such as – what happens if such paths are taken? What place is there for client choice? Which approach best suits which type of client? And, perhaps most importantly of all, how do we need to adapt each approach to best suit the individual circumstances?

Read and apply an article or a chapter from a book

Similar to the above case, a learner can read a particular chapter from a book in preparation for the following supervision. The task can be varied – applying the issues to an individual case, reflecting on its relevance to the setting, critiquing the evidence and its method. Novels which provide obvious lines of debate can also be used, for example, *The Curious Incident of the Dog in the Night Time* by Mark Haddon tells the story of a boy with Asperger's syndrome as he tries to understand a complicated world.

Knowledge mapping

learners can list different areas of knowledge that apply to the setting in which they are working. Learners may wish to think of the areas of

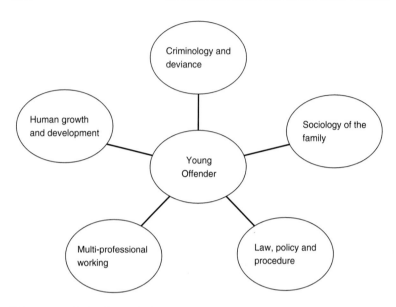

Diagram 6.5   Knowledge mapping

curriculum they have engaged with so far. These can be arranged on a piece of paper or flipchart to form a spider-gram (Diagram 6.5).

   This physical representation allows learners to 'reify' theoretical knowledge and make it real. It also allows them to begin to breakdown the relationship between different areas of theory, competing ideas and so on. More fundamentally, as learners we begin to sense the complexity of clients' situations and the body of knowledge we need to bring to bear on an individual situation. This can seem more manageable when broken down in this form. It can also be a useful tool to breakdown the lazy interpretations of eclecticism. The spider-gram enables us to explore each area separately while keeping a central focus on the client.

Diaries, learning logs and journals

There are numerous versions of these concepts but their essence remains the same – some ongoing account of what learners have been thinking in response to their work setting. This can be angled towards theory to practice issues, communication and discrimination – any issues that learners and enablers may agree merits further reflection. More commonly, the account may simply be a reminder, related to the gathering of evidence for portfolios, of the learner's activities. By their nature, such diaries and learning logs are not usually confined to the learner and can often be brought to supervision, but enablers need to ensure that this point is clear at the outset. Whilst similar to diaries and learning logs, learning journals have a more expansive approach and often a more creative slant. Creative learners might write about practice from a third perspective to promote understanding or compose an unsent letter to someone to free feelings and emotions. Journals can also contain reflections on books and articles read, or hold lists such as things learners think they are good at, things they think they need to know more about and so forth. 'Stepping stones' activities encourage journal writers to list their memories of events in chronological order. There is tremendous creative and imaginative scope with journals (Moon, 1999). However, authors need to ensure that they record their thoughts in a useful manner for the purpose intended.

ACTIVITY

To develop skills in reflective writing within journals

Excerpt from a reflective journal

I spent the morning shadowing another worker (K) to observe what she did. She was very skilled and I learnt a lot from watching her. I was especially impressed by the way she dealt sensitively with Mr C's complaints about the nurses. I felt that he had been relieved of his frustration without K getting drawn into criticising colleagues. I can try to use the same sort of skills in my work.

1. What do you think is missing from this?
2. What sort of things might have been recorded that would make it a more valuable learning tool?
3. Rewrite the excerpt.

Source: Adapted from Beale, 2005.

In completing the activity, learners should be raising their awareness of the need for detail and illustration when referring to things such as 'skills' – what sort of skills were used and in what way? Experienced practitioners often find this issue particularly hard – often for the very reason that they have ceased to reflect on their professional practice sometime ago and have (perhaps understandably) moved into 'doing' and managing rather than reflecting.

Tape record a client interview and discuss

Provided that permission has been sought, tape recording can gather important and interesting primary data about the learner's performance – without the stress of an enabler observing every syllable and twitch. Learners may tape an interview and construct a theoretical understanding of their intervention in terms of language, communication, social work method, policy and procedure, empowering practice and so on. This can be a process of self learning (and surprise) as learners listen to themselves and reflect. Enablers can model good practice by providing a tape they 'made earlier'.

Critical incident analysis

This activity requires the identification of a critical incident – something that affected the learner or enabler. This can be a professional scenario (an interview that went wrong, a tense moment in a staff meeting) or perhaps something that happened outside of the professional role (a disagreement with a friend). Obviously this should only be shared at a level with which learners and enablers are comfortable. Either through personal reflection or supervision discussion, try to unravel what happened in the incident – expose it to critical reflection.

Jan Fook is an advocate of critical incident analysis and constructs a more in-depth form of the model depicted in Diagram 6.6, asking for reflection on emerging themes, differing perspectives and interpretations, assumptions and theories of power which is discussed in the chapter on supervision (Fook, 2002).

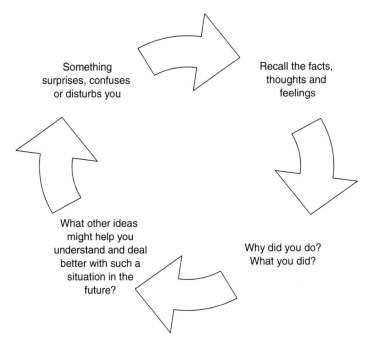

Diagram 6.6   Critical incident analysis

Reflection and Profession

We wish to conclude this chapter with some observations on the nature of reflection, profession and professional identity. Little of the literature informing social work is written from the social worker's professional point of view and too often the literature fails to acknowledge the difficulties in finding time to step outside of the pressures to simply get the work done. The 'swampy lowland' where the real reflective practitioners work has many organisational demands that may well conflict with how the social worker would choose to construct the professional task. Indeed, organisational cultures may well conflict at quite deep levels with professional cultures. At a basic level the professional worker's emphasis may be placed on the quality of the contact with service users, whilst the organisation may place a greater emphasis on the quantity of contact or its level of compliance with procedure. We are all familiar with 'needs-led' versus 'resource-led' assessment. Authors such as Etzioni talk of the basic incompatibility of the authority of professional knowledge and the authority of administrative hierarchy (Etzioni, 1969). As learners and enablers in social work settings we might reflect on what aspects of professional practice we tend to reflect on – what aspects of knowledge are given the most priority and why? Reflective practice, for all its obvious merits, takes place within a professional and organisational context which has obvious political tensions. It is interesting to compare other professions that exist within organisations and the relative power differences that accrue between professional knowledge and organisational demands (the medical professional within the NHS is a typical illustration). Should the (expert) professional have complete control over the decision-making process – or are there significant merits to procedurally driven interventions? Authors on professional identity such as Friedson have commented on the need to maintain an (uneasy?) balance between the two as pure expressions of each are problematic: 'Professional failure is marked by the dissolution into pure discretion, while administrative failure is marked by the petrification of forms' (Friedson, 1994, p. 70).

Thus, if social workers are simply free to do as they choose the profession is in danger of falling into a chaotic state, whilst the converse for the organisation is the weight of policy, form filling and procedure solidifying movement into stone. It is in neither party's interest to exert too much power over the other in this analysis. Reflection, for the worker, needs to engage with this dynamic. Clearly it becomes vital for the profession to ensure that enough of the 'right' knowledge and power is exerted in our working life. Perhaps this is where we can place another missing piece of the jigsaw of reflective practice. In following this line of thought, we are not only acknowledging the need for reflecting together within the professional arena, as Schön always suggested, but realising that this is taking place within a *contested* arena that relates closely to who we are and how we think of ourselves. As we consider the issue of theory into practice, the need to retain a critical perspective on knowledge and power becomes evident. All understanding of practice, interventions, learning and enabling derives from ideas (theories) of one sort or another – whether it be from formal classroom types of learning, the experiences we gather in our personal and professional lives, the value base of ourselves, our professional group or our organisations (Fisher and Somerton, 2000). 'What matters is that all these things are made explicit and thought about rather than implicit and never questioned' (Fisher and Somerton, 2000, p. 399).

Within this chapter we have considered a brief overview of the idea of reflective practice and some of its main thinkers, notably Dewy, Schön and Friere. We have seen how the concept has developed over time and, in particular, the importance of ensuring that reflexivity becomes an aspect of our approach, as learners and enablers, to reflective practice. The activities selected in this chapter have attempted to provide some avenues to explore the links between theory and practice with a reflexive dimension. Finally, we have considered the professional and organisational context we inhabit as social workers and the impact that can have on reflective practice. Reflective practice clearly has much to deliver in its potential to transform ourselves, our ideas and our world. The ability of enablers to work with learners in developing reflective skills and techniques remains, perhaps, the central function of supervision. Reflective practice seems to work best within a positive dialogue that takes account of service user's needs: 'Theory should be a guide to be used together with clients to explore, understand and transform the social world in which we live together' (Payne, 1998, p. 136).

ACTIVITY

To think about thinking

Work with at least one other professional worker in your agency on the following questions:

What forms and types of knowledge are important to the organisation and the profession – are they the same? Are they in competition? Who is winning? Is the balance appropriate from the professional point of view? The service users view?

What about the culture of the organisation and the culture of the professionals within it? Are they the same? Is one more dominant? How do I know this?

How does this impact on service delivery?

Key Learning Points

- Reflective practice and reflexive practice are key concepts for the learner and enabler, but should be approached critically as such.
- Reflective practice helps the practitioner deal with uncertainty and complexity.
- Reflective practice skills can be developed using different models.
- Reflective practice should not be limited to social work practice, but should include our profession, its knowledge base, the organisational structures it inhabits and so on – we should always question everything.

CHAPTER 7

Evidencing and Assessing Competence

This chapter will consider the purposes of assessment and the principles for undertaking a fair assessment. Assessment methods and the principles of constructive feedback will be discussed. When social workers undergoing training to become enablers are asked to give a definition of assessment invariably they refer to social work assessment. Their understanding of the processes they go through to make an assessment on a service user can easily be transferred to the 'enabling' arena: 'Assessment in education can be thought of as occurring whenever one person in some kind of interaction, direct or indirect, with another, is conscious of obtaining and interpreting information about the knowledge and understanding, or abilities and attitudes of that other person' (Rowntree, 1987, p. 4).

Purpose of Assessment

Cree and Macaulay (2000) argue that students learn according to how they are tested. If they are tested for recall of facts then that is what they will learn; if they are tested for their ability to analyse relationships then that is what they will learn. Whatever the method of facilitating learning used, if the students are tested by conventional means they will reproduce conventional learning. Entwhistle (1996) suggests that deep learning occurs when learners are able to understand ideas for themselves, and it is fostered by open and collaborative assessment systems. However, restrictive and overloaded assessment systems lead to a surface learning approach or a strategic approach where learners concentrate on only the learning outcomes likely to be tested rather than the wider learning objectives. So the move from written examinations, tutor-led assignments to more course work, student-led assignments and an emphasis on competencies rather than content, which has been taking place in higher education since the 1970s, should facilitate a deep learning approach.

According to Miller, Imrie and Cox (1998) assessment in higher education has two purpose:

1. To direct and enhance student learning.
2. To confirm learning outcomes and maintain standards.

Other writers including Evans (1999) and Brown and Knight (1994) would argue that the purposes of assessment in higher and particularly professional education are as follows:

1. To select appropriate candidates for the profession or to confirm achievement that an individual has met the standards of a qualified practitioner.
2. To identify areas of learning need within individual learners.
3. To provide learners with feedback on their progress and achievements.
4. To give learners confidence in their ability.
5. To motivate learners to continue to learn.
6. To gain knowledge to help shape any future learning opportunities.

Evans (1999) argues that the first function does not sit comfortably with the others. Informing a learner that he or she is not making the grade for the profession may lead to anxiety and a breakdown in communication between learner and enabler so that learning falters. Conversely concentration on the learning and development needs of a learner may mean that an enabler is unwilling to judge the learner in relation to whether or not he or she meet the standards of the profession. Certainly in the social work profession the concentration of both enabling and assessment functions within the one role of practice teacher can lead to conflict for that individual. Some professions deal with this dilemma by separating the functions of assessment and enabling between different people. Thus the assessment is not influenced unduly by the relationship between assessor and learner. The enabler could be influenced by the progress the learners have made, the effort they have made or what is at stake for them personally should they not make the grade. When it comes to assessment this may mean that they have difficulty in failing a learner in order to safeguard the standards of the profession. Reviewing the impact on service users and colleagues of social workers who are incompetent may help address this dilemma. Using a range of evidence from sources that can be viewed by a third party may help share decision making.

Types of Assessment

Assessment can be categorised according to purpose:

- *Diagnostic assessment* to identify learning needs and the types of learning strategies needed to meet the learner's style.
- *Formative assessment* undertaken during a learning programme to give learners feedback in order to motivate them, give them confidence by identifying strengths and help them focus on areas to develop by identifying weaknesses.
- *Summative assessment* at the end of a learning programme to make a judgement on whether or not the learning outcomes have been met.

Learners should be clear about the purpose of each assessment. They should not confuse formative assessment, which is an aid to learning, with summative assessment, which will decide certification for qualification, and thus be the gate for entry to a profession.

The two main bases on which assessments are made are criterion-based assessment where a judgement is made against specific predetermined criteria and norm-based assessment where a learner is compared with a norm established by peers. In criterion-based assessment all learners who meet the criteria will pass. In norm-based assessment the number of learners who pass at different levels will depend on a normal distribution curve. This means that learner's results will depend on the capabilities of the peers. Learners on a social work education programme will be assessed against the criteria of National Occupational Standards. As we have seen elsewhere these standards are open to the interpretation by both leaner and enabler.

Assessments will in practice also be norm referenced, in that judgements will be made against what is generally accepted as the standard in the particular agency where the learner is placed. Another norm, which will be employed, is the standard of the enabler's own practice. This may be linked to agency norms but not always. According to Evans (1999) practice teachers have a higher commitment to professional standards than other staff. One problem here is whether the expectations of these practice teachers are of qualified staff rather than learners in training. With experience the enabler/assessor may be able to judge where the standard should be set but there are clear problems about whether or not the standards of different assessors are the same. In this way the difference between norm-based assessment and criterion-based assessment becomes blurred. An enabler/assessor may well be able to see that learners have progressed in their practice but this still begs the question whether or not their practice is 'good enough.' For example, when a learner is being assessed on his or her communication skills the assessor will need to make a decision about whether they are assessing; the learner on the information conveyed, the method in which it was conveyed or indeed what information was actually received. All these may be very different. Some assessors may decide that the first two are adequate for a beginning social worker, others that all three are necessary for effective communication. Although criteria in the form of National Occupational Standards are helpful, they do not avoid differences of opinion.

Raelin (2000) argues that learning in the work base arises from solving problems and learning from experience. It is centred on the reflection on work practices. According to Crisp and Lister (2003) assessment methods used in the work base need to encourage the development of reflective and critical learning as well as enabling students to demonstrate the acquisition of required knowledge and skills. Fortunately, within the National Occupational Standards for Social Work, Key Role 6 is 'reflect on and continue to develop your professional practice', therefore, any assessor cannot avoid taking this into consideration.

The Process of Assessment

According to Cree and Macaulay (2000) there are six steps in the assessment process. These are as follows:

1. Determine what is to be assessed, that is, what constitutes competence.
2. Design the means of assessment and the criteria.

3. Assess by applying the criteria.
4. Interpret the results and decide what they tell us about student progress.
5. Give feedback to the learner.
6. Use the feedback to improve the teaching.

Donley and Napper (1999) include more steps which refer to sharing the learning outcomes with learners, collecting evidence from learners and discussing the results with learners. This approach has a closer resonance with the values of social work which would include within any assessment process the viewpoint of those being assessed.

In terms of learning on a social work education programme, learners will have a judgement made of their competence, as this is part of education for qualification. This can feel disempowering if not undertaken in an anti-oppressive way. The enabler can empower learners by encouraging them to take responsibility for their own learning. Including them in the assessment process is critical to this function. The *Concise Oxford Dictionary* includes 'estimate the value of' in its definition of assessment. However, assessing learning outcomes in adult learners is about measuring changes individuals have made in their knowledge skills and values, and not about estimating the value or worth of an individual. Yet many of the learners in social work practice particularly those undergoing initial qualification training may have had just such an experience of assessment in the past. It is possible that these feelings may be reawakened when they realise that they are to be assessed on their competence in the work base. Assessors too may have personal experiences of assessment techniques which have left them with strong feelings about the process. Thus assessment could become an interpersonal minefield where the participants find themselves enmeshed in one of the roles of the 'drama triangle' which lead to game playing (Donley and Napper, 1999; Morrison, 2002) (Diagram 7.1). The three roles of the triangle are victim, persecutor and rescuer.

The learner as victim sees the assessment as unfair by creating comparisons with others. The effect is for the learner to disengage from the process and thus not benefit from any feedback he or she receives. The assessor as victim avoids undertaking assessment lest it shows up poor teaching techniques or requires him or her to give negative feedback to the learner. The learner gains nothing from the experience.

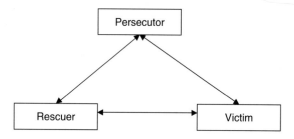

Diagram 7.1   Drama Triangle

The learner as rescuer does not give a clear picture in his or her feedback in order to protect the assessor; therefore learning is again hindered. The assessor as rescuer only gives positive feedback to learners to avoid hurting their feelings. Thus the learner has no pointers to help them improve their practice. The learners as persecutors blame the assessor for flaws in the assessment or teaching process so that they do not have to take responsibility for their own practice. The assessor as persecutor uses methods that the learner finds difficult or gives all negative feedback so that the learner feels overwhelmed by his or her inadequacies and is unable to learn. Recognition of the game playing would hopefully help stop it. However, it is preferable to use strategies that will help avoid becoming enmeshed in the triangle in the first place. These strategies should include making the process of assessment clear to the learner. Assessment processes should be discussed with the learner and their preferences accommodated where possible. The right to reply to an assessor's assessment is also important for empowering the learner. If assessors shares formative assessment with learners, encourage them to give a reasoned view of their progress and include the learner's view in the final judgement, then learners should feel that the process is inclusive.

Assessment should be built into the learning programme from the start so that it is always on the agenda. Early in the learning programme a discussion could take place about the learner's previous experience of assessments so that assessors can offer reassurance and acknowledge the learner's vulnerability. Discussion could also take place about the different purposes of assessment so that the learner is aware of the value of assessment. Learners should be clear when assessment is diagnostic, formative or summative. Advance warning of when assessment will take place will allow learners to be prepared.

If a wide range of assessment tools is used then this will not give unfair advantages to specific sorts of learners. Learners should be familiar with the criteria used for assessment and included in a discussion about what sorts of evidence would demonstrate competence. Some competence-based assessments include both positive and negative indicators of competence so that learners know what is unacceptable as well as what is acceptable. Including learners in such a discussion could help them become aware of the standards against which they are being assessed. Feedback should be clear, honest and include the learner's views. This information sharing and inclusion of the learner within the assessment process is an important part of empowering the learner.

The Principles of Assessment

There are six overarching principles which should underpin any assessment procedure (Donley and Napper, 1999; Evans, 1999; Brown and Knight, 1994). The first principle of reliability is concerned with the consistency of judgements that are made when assessing evidence and is probably the most difficult. An assessment is considered to be reliable if two or more assessors agree with each other, if any one assessor comes to the same judgement on different occasions or if different assessment methods confirm the same judgement. Another phrase used to refer to this sort of reliability is 'triangulation' (Evans, 1999). In academic institutions it is thought that discussing findings, resolving differences and seeking a common view often sorts out differences between assessors. However, Cree and Macaulay (2000) argue that there is no real objectivity or standardisation between marks given in different universities, different faculties within the same university and different markers within the same department. Assessors are often judging the work of several students at any one time and so form a judgement against the norm of the group. They may have hundreds of examples of work on which to base a judgement. This is rarely possible in assessment of learners in the workplace. Even if someone is acting as assessor to several learners at one time the total number is not likely to be great. Assessors are often working in isolation and judging very different pieces of practice, so they do not have a norm to work against until they build up some degree of experience over time. In order to improve the reliability of the assessment Evans (2000) argues that several people should be involved in the assessment. This could include line managers, who are used to dealing with a variety of staff at different levels of expertise, so that they have some norms against which to assess the learner. They should be used to assess aspects of the learner's work in which they may be involved by virtue of their role, such as the learner's ability to follow agency procedures or advocate for resources. Other practitioners who may have been working with the learner in a specific area of practice, possibly by co-working could be involved. Administrative staff may have a particular contribution to make about the learner's ability to work within organisational practices. Other significant people to include in assessment are the service users with whom the learner is working. They are the only people who can say how the service offered by the learner is experienced. This needs to be done very carefully so that the service user knows why they are being involved and what is expected of them. The feedback may need to be sought such that the service users can remain anonymous to the service particularly if they are concerned that their view of the learner may impact on the service they are offered. Service user feedback will be dealt with in more detail later in this chapter.

The second principle concerns validity. Assessment is valid if it measures what it is intended to measure. A written account by learners on how they undertook a piece of work with a service user is a common way of assessing competence required by social work education programmes. As evidence of the learner's competence in practice it may not be particularly valid. Learners may have misinterpreted what was happening in the user's life, and may have been unaware of crucial aspects of their practice or even changed the account from what they actually did to what they should have done. The account might however be evidence of their knowledge relevant to the situation, their understanding of the role of the agency, their ability to identify the values on which they operate and their capacity to reflect. A more valid way of assessing practice performance is to actually observe the learner undertaking the piece of work with the service user. This may be easy in some settings where joint work is common or work is generally undertaken in full view of a number of other people such as residential or day-care settings. If this is the case, the assessors have to be careful that they can distinguish between what the learner does in the situation and what other people do, otherwise they may end up making an assessment on the skills of another. In other settings where lone working is the norm it may be more difficult.

The written word may be a more reliable assessment in that more than one assessor can access the material and agree on a judgement, but it could be considered less valid. However, the practice performance will be valid in testing the learner's ability to work directly with service users but not necessarily reliable. Validity is currently seen as more important than reliability (Brown and Knight, 1994). The key thing to remember is that competence in practice includes work undertaken directly with service users and indirect work performed on behalf of the service user. It includes all internal processes, such as linking theory to practice and reflecting on practice as well as external behaviours. In order to capture all these elements of competence, an assessor needs a repertoire of assessment methods. Using a range of assessment methods and involving several people within the assessment process should assist both validity and reliability of the overall assessment of the learner.

Authenticity is the third principle. Assessment tools should be such that the work which is produced comes from the person who is undergoing assessment. In the days of word-processed written work, this cannot always be guaranteed. Generally students in higher education have to declare that an assignment is their own work although this relies on their honesty and it would be difficult to disprove. Although the increasing use of Internet search engines are making this easier, it is easy to authenticate a piece of directly observed work with a service user by an assessor who knows the learner. More difficult again is a written piece about practical work that the learner has carried out. As social work tutors we have found students who elaborate the account of their practice or even produce a fictional account. For this reason it is necessary for written accounts of practice to be authenticated by someone who can vouch for the practice. An assessor who knows the learner's practice may introduce an element of bias into the assessment of written work as he or she sometimes uses this knowledge to read more into the written word than is actually written, but it does counter the problem of authenticity.

Fourth, an assessment should be relatively easy to administer and to judge. If assessors have to spend large amounts of time administering the assessment, then they will have less time to deal with the results.

The fifth principle concerns fairness. Assessment tools should not advantage one group of people over another. Clearly, to be competent as a social worker it is necessary to provide coherent accounts of practice which are evidence based. Practitioners may be able to articulate the evidence base for their practice but may not be able to convey it in written form so well. Learners who are good at writing about their practice may not be as good at presenting it orally or visually. Practitioners who can write comprehensive reports may be less good at conveying information in person or over the telephone. Not everyone can excel at everything, so it is important to use a range of assessment tools that focus on different skills.

The sixth principle is sufficiency and refers to the issue that each assessor will need to be satisfied that the evidence he or she has gained from the assessment is enough to judge that the learner is competent. Evans (2000) identifies three factors that need to be considered under sufficiency. Frequency refers to the number of times a learner must demonstrate a particular competence. If learners do it satisfactorily on three occasions but not on a fourth, does this mean that they are competent or not? Some competence-based assessment frameworks indicate how many demonstrations are necessary, but this is not so in social work. Range indicates the number of different circumstances in which a learner should demonstrate competence. The key roles in the National Occupational Standards refer to work with individuals, groups, families, carers and communities. To be qualified are learners expected to demonstrate their competence with all these categories and then, within each category a range of difference, for example, older people, teenagers, young children, people of both genders, all ethnic groups and those with different levels of ability? It is certainly not clear from the standards what the expectations are in terms of range. Student social workers are only expected to work with two different service user groups in different settings; so they could not possibly cover all these categories. The assessor is then left with the dilemma of deciding what range of settings is sufficient. The third factor referred to by Evans (2000) is level. The National Occupational Standards apply to what is expected of a social worker both recently qualified and some years into their professional career. So level is not easy to determine from the standards. It is left to the assessor to decide. Some social work degree programmes expect all key roles to be evidenced in all practice placements. This leaves the assessors in each placement with the dilemma about the level required at that point in learning.

All these issues pose dilemmas for the assessor and point to the need to have support in the role from others in a similar position.

Feedback

Feedback to learners on their performance has a major role in the learning process (Evans, 2000; Hincliff, 1999). Feedback is only useful if it helps learners to develop their practice. A useful mnemonic for the principles of feedback is SCORE.

- **S**pecific
- **C**lear
- **O**wned
- **R**egular
- **E**ven handed.

Learners need feedback that is specific in referring to what they have done well and the areas for improvement. Saying to learners that they did well tells them nothing. Conversely, saying that they did well to listen to the service user so intently when there were so many distractions tells them what they did well. Adding that it might have been useful to avoid some of the distractions and asking how they might be able to do this gives them some ideas about what they could do in the future.

Feedback from the assessor is their own view of the situation. It is therefore important to make this clear by using 'I' phrases. 'I thought that the service user looked confused when you referred to the different possible benefits available to them.' In the spirit of empowerment it is important to get the learner's view of the situation. The assessor may have misunderstood the learner's intentions or may not have been aware that the information he or she considered missing had been covered at another time. Including the learner in the discussion during feedback can rectify this. Asking the service user whether the information was clear to them may be the one way to be sure.

Feedback should refer to the things which can be changed in the learner's practice. Telling them that they intimidated the children in the nursery because they are so tall is not helpful unless the assessor goes on to ask the learners how they might overcome the possible effects of their size on little children.

Feedback is often referred to as a sandwich with the areas for improvement being sandwiched between the areas of strength. Discussions with many sorts of learners on feedback have led us to qualify this idea. Several learners have told us that they do not listen to the praise because they are always waiting for the *'BUT ...'* which inevitably follows it. Some learners have been subject to so much condemnation in the past that they fail to see anything positive in their performance. Others have always succeeded in everything they do, and so find traumatic any suggestions that they may not be perfect. A good discipline is to try to avoid the word 'but' and 'although' as some learners dismiss all the positive comments that precede these qualifiers. It might also be useful to ask the learner how he or she would like to receive feedback.

Often in their eagerness to help the learner improve their practice the assessor limits the emphasis on praise and concentrates on the areas for improvement. Hinchliff (1999) and Evans (2000) both express the view that learners generally need more praise than they get. Identification of weaknesses is not enough to lead to an improvement in practice. The assessor needs to engage learners in a discussion about how they can improve. The balance can become skewed either towards too much criticism or too much praise. The latter is a distinct possibility where the enabler is also the assessor and has developed a close relationship with the learner. They may take justifiable pride in the learner's accomplishments and may feel unable to focus on areas for development.

Assessment Methods

Gray (2001) points out that assessment methods in work-based learning tend to differ from those used in more traditional learning settings. They require more of a problem solving approach and a more involvement of learners in the assessment process. A key aspect of supervision is the translation of activity or practice into evidence of competence. With the large number of requirements to be met in the National Occupational Standards (NOS) this can feel burdensome and bureaucratic. Nevertheless, they do have to be met and this can result in the learner thinking that they are more important than the agency activity. The following simple guidelines may help to avoid the feeling that 'competencies rule ok'.

1. Learners and enablers need to spend some time considering the NOS in isolation from discussions about the learners' practice. They need to come to a common shared understanding of what phrases mean. Handbooks from social work education programmes may have further guidance and can be informative.

2.   Collecting evidence for competence can be done in whatever way suits the learner best, for example, computer files and log books. Recording of evidence should be done on a regular basis; it is often useful to have this as a standing supervision agenda item.

3.   Although it is usually the learner's role to provide the evidence, the enabler will often become a facilitator, helping the learner to do this.

4.   Understand that 'evidence' takes a wealth of different forms. Direct evidence is concrete material such as observation reports, case file material (anonymised), meeting minutes and so on. Indirect evidence includes reports by the learner, discussions, assignments and so on. Different social work education programmes will require different sorts of evidence but generally the bulk of the evidence within any portfolio is indirect evidence.

Self-assessment

Brown and Knight (1994) argue that self-evaluative skills are important in developing students' awareness of their own abilities which lead to more effective learning. Part of becoming a lifelong learner is the ability to be reflective. The importance of self-assessment evidence is what it reveals about the learners' thought processes and the values which underpin their work. Learners can be encouraged to keep a reflective log or diary about each day in the work base. They will need guidance on what to include, as the purpose of the log is more than recording events. The log should include a short description of significant events, reflection on their feelings, identification of learning, any extra knowledge they need to make sense of the events and how they are going to take any learning from these events forward into their practice. They can also be encouraged to make an assessment on their own practice in relation to the learning outcomes that have been set. The log can be used (with permission) in supervision sessions or to help compile pieces of work for their portfolio. Some learners may be over generous in rating their own performance, while others over critical; both these will help the enabler understand the standards and expectations which the learners have of themselves. They can then use these to compare standards and expectations of the practice agency in supervision. If facilities are available, some learners may wish to record their logs in the form of a video diary. The ability to self-assess is important for any professional post-qualification. It is unlikely that they will be assessed by others in a way which will benefit their practice once they are qualified unless they undertake formal post-qualification education or unless their employer has a mentoring system for staff. Models considered in the chapter on reflective practice will be useful to the enabler in encouraging self-assessment in the learner.

The following is a list of activities which can be used to allow the learners to demonstrate their competence and generate evidence. The activities are similar to those identified as teaching/learning techniques in the chapter on Creating and Using Learning Opportunities because they have a dual function. Learners will need to be very clear when a strategy is being used for learning, which may include formative assessment, and when it is being used for summative assessment.

Work-based products

This is a term from National Vocational qualifications and refers to pieces of work that learners produce in the course of their day-to-day activities. Enablers/assessors may wish to use these as evidence of competence. These may include entries in agency records, written reports on individuals or circumstances, letters, e-mails, telephone conversations or assessment records.

Case studies, case presentations

It is likely that learners on social work education programmes will have to produce some sort of a detailed account of work with one or more service user. This will include reference to appropriate legislation, agency procedures, theories which inform assessment and the methods used to work with the service user. It will also include a reflection on the process. Enablers may not want or need as much detail as that expected in a written assignment by the education programme, but they may find the basic model useful. This gives learners an opportunity to explain their working practices. The information could be presented in a written format, through a verbal presentation or any other way that capitalises on the learner's creative abilities.

Action plans

Learners can be encouraged to produce short action plans in whatever format they wish to illustrate their plans for work with particular service users. These can be useful to consider their ability to assess need and plan action and review the progress of ongoing work through supervision.

Discussions and skill rehearsal

Time in supervision can be usefully spent discussing aspects of the learner's work within the work base. Where learning opportunities have not been as readily available as expected, some of these discussions can centre around 'what if' scenarios. Learners can be encouraged to think about how they would need to change their practice if the service user they are working with had communication difficulties or was from an ethnic minority or was unwilling to engage with the learner. Skill rehearsal could be employed to see if the learners can rehearse some of these changes that they have articulated. Skill rehearsal gives the enabler a chance to assess whether the learner is safe to be let loose on service user.

Projects

The learner can often make significant contributions to an agency by investigating the needs of service users or their views about the service offered and then making suggestions to improve service delivery. Such projects are useful vehicles to assess their competence. With the inclusion in the key roles of competence in group work skills, some agencies are using students to take the opportunity to set up group work projects which they have not had the resources for in the past. There are a vast range of projects, which learners could be encouraged to undertake to benefit the agency in which they are placed.

Direct observation of practice

Actually observing a learner working with service users either in the same room as them or via video is a good method of assessing competence. It does however need careful preparation. The service users need to agree to the observation and understand that it is the learner who is being observed not them. Learner and assessor together will need to agree what is involved in the work and what will be assessed. Agreement should be reached about whether or not the assessor is going to intervene if the learner needs help, or whether the service users address their remarks to the assessor. If the observation is primarily for assessment, intervention would be unlikely, but if it is a learning opportunity it might be very helpful to the learner for the enabler to intervene. Either scenario is possible but clarity is important to prevent uncertainty and resentment if expectations are not met. Evans (2000) refers to this as agreeing upon the ground rules. He argues that this is necessary due to the unpredictable nature of prac-tice. Both will need to know the contingency plans if things change during the observation. Arrangements should be made about when and in what form feedback will take place. Learners should be encour-aged to make an assessment of their own performance in line with encouraging self-assessment. The discussion, which follows this assess-ment by the student, may be most effective as soon as possible after the observation in order to give both participants the best opportunity to remember detail. It is also useful to consider the observation again when both parties have had some time to reflect on the learner's practice. The use of video or audio tapes is a great way of encouraging self-assessment, as this allows learners to relive the experience and con-centrate on their performance rather than the service users' needs.

Reports by service users

The views of service users about what they want from social workers are now included in statements at the beginning of the NOS. There are issues about the capacity of some service users to give meaningful feedback, for example, service users with severe learning disabilities or mental health problems, or young children, but this does not mean that these groups of service users should be excluded. It might take more time and require some creative ways of seeking the feedback, but this should not mean that feedback is not sought in these circumstances. There are other issues about whether reluctant service users or service users who do not receive the service which they request will be able to separate out the performance of the learner from the response of the service. Similarly, there are issues about who seeks the feedback and how this may have a potential bias on the outcome. Some social work education programmes undertake to elicit the feedback as this is one stage removed from service delivery. In these situations there are issues about access to service users and how they get chosen. Also, if the feedback is in written form it may depend on the service user being motivated enough to complete and return a form through the post. Edwards (2003) in a research project on this topic found that practice teachers felt that service users should be included in all forms of assessment and so service user feedback should be sought throughout the learner's period of practice. The inclusion of the service user opinion during a direct observation of practice by the practice teacher was seen as a useful way of recording different views on the same piece of work. This is an example of 'triangulation' as explained above. Specific areas were noted which were particularly relevant for the service user to comment on and these include the areas identified at the beginning of the NOS. The issue seems not to be that service users' views should be included, but how this is managed in a consistent way. In a study by Shennan in 1998, the barriers to seeking feedback from service users identified by practice teachers were around time, their own organisational ability and the lack of an agreed method. Since that time the Social Care Institute for Excellence have produced a resource guide which identifies ways of including service users in all aspects of social work education (SCIE, 2003). The guide makes suggestions that feedback should be sought through a semi-structured format which is geared to those areas identified as important to service users. The guide suggests that this can be done verbally by the enabler/assessor of practice or student, and the service user can either complete it by responding verbally to the questions or in writing. The guide suggests that where there are communication difficulties, the enabler and learner together should devise appropriate ways of overcoming the difficulties. Strong recommendations are made that the learner and enabler should together pick the service user chosen to give feedback. It would then be the enabler's role to translate service user's comments into evidence of competence or areas for development. Service user feedback is one part of a range of assessment strategies that an enabler can use.

The issue about what an enabler does when the service user feedback is at odds with other sources of evidence is no different from the issue they face when any source of evidence is at odds with other sources. The enabler will need to weigh the evidence alongside all sources and make a judgement accordingly. One response might be to seek out more service user feedback in order to counteract any bias from the service users or allay the fear that the learner may be treating service users oppressively. Avoidance of the involvement of service users because of potential problems is not acceptable particularly when several of the studies done (Edwards, 2003; SCIE, 2003; Shennan, 1998) have indicated that the majority of enablers undertaking service user feedback have found the process straightforward.

Competency-based assignments

Most social work education programmes, both at qualifying and post-qualifying level, expect students to write about practice. This sort of assignment is very different from those they may have written under purely academic structures. An academic essay usually involves the construction of critical arguments around propositions. A competency-based assignment is fundamentally about the provision of evidence that corresponds to the competencies which the learner needs to demonstrate. Practice should be at the heart of these assignments usually including specific illustrations of their work. The assignment will be full of 'I' statements. They should be encouraged to be specific about their actions and so on. Making statements such as 'I worked in an anti oppressive manner with this person' is not satisfactory. They will need to say exactly how they did this giving examples. The competencies to be covered can be used as a plan for the assignment. They can often be grouped together and connections made between them. It is rare that competencies can be evidenced in a single sentence. They are best evidenced in pages or paragraphs that consider the nature of the competency and provide evidence of practice and reflection which directly relate to it. Generally, all competencies have equal weightage and all must be met; therefore learners should avoid concentrating on one particular competence to the exclusion of others. Learners should include in their assignments the knowledge which justifies their actions. This will include theory, research, legislation and agency policy. Most competency-based assignments also require learners to demonstrate critical reflection of their practice as an integral part of the assignment.

Once the assignment is complete many social work education programmes expect that the enabler is involved somehow in the marking. This may just be validation of the work on which the assignment is written indicating that it is up to the usual standards of the agency or it may be to contribute an academic mark. The former is relatively easy; the latter not so. Unless they have a strong and recent academic background, most enablers find the idea of giving a percentage mark to a piece of work horrifying. They worry that their knowledge of theory is not comprehensive enough, and they are not really in a position to judge the academic quality of a piece of work. Most enablers are only seeing their learner's piece of work and so do not have norms against which to judge. Joint marking should mean just that. Both markers should bring appropriate expertise to the job. Social Work Education Programmes will often help by providing workshops to assist enablers in this task. These workshops will concentrate on the use of marking criteria and relative weightings given for each criteria. Grade descriptors will tell the marker what is expected for a pass standard, for a high standard and so on.

On the basis of what they have discussed with the learner, what they have observed, what they have heard from service users and colleagues, and what they have read, the enabler will need to make a recommendation about whether or not the learner demonstrates competence. The enabler's report will be considered alongside the evidence produced in the portfolio by the learner. The enabler's report and recommendation should fit with and complement the evidence presented by the learner. In order to 'pass' or be deemed competent, the learner will need to meet all criteria required. Compensation between criteria is not allowed. An assessment panel consisting of practice people and academics will generally consider the evidence. If the learners do not meet all criteria, or if they consider that the evidence is not of good enough quality then they may ask for more evidence, and evidence to be rewritten so that it is clearer or require the learner to undertake more practice.

The portfolio

Social work education programmes usually have prescribed assessment methods which the student has to complete. This is often a portfolio. In general usage the term portfolio refers to a collection of the best work of an individual. The person compiling the portfolio picks what he or she want to include. In social work, the education programme generally prescribes the structure of the portfolio. The learner usually chooses the pieces of work within that structure. The systems, which underpin the use of portfolios for assessment, vary enormously. Some are assessed by individuals, some by panels and others through viva voce. 'Some systems will require little more than written assignments while others will ask for a true portfolio of materials; that is, a collection of evidence using a variety of media' (Doel, Sawdon and Morrison, 2002, p. 75).

It is important to be clear about how the sources of evidence in a portfolio can be protected, therefore issues of confidentiality must be considered. The important factor in the portfolio is that it contains the voice of the learner which is not given through another, such as the supervisor (Doel and Shardlow, 1998). The portfolio should not just include evidence of specific skills but also evidence that learners can reflect on their practice and explain the purpose of their work. There is very little critical analysis of the use of portfolios in practice (Taylor, Thomas and Sage, 1999). Although the summative assessment takes the form of a portfolio this does not mean that assessor/enablers cannot use other tools such as those identified above for diagnostic and formative assessment.

Key Learning Points

- It is important that both learner and enabler are clear about the process and purpose of any assessment which is undertaken.
- Assessment in social work is subjective, but there are ways to reduce the subjectivity and bias.
- Careful attention needs to be paid about feelings and communication in assessment, otherwise it can be experienced as oppressive.
- Including assessment in the role of enabler can affect that relationship.
- Activities in the work base can be used both as learning and assessment methods. Learners will need to know whether they are being used for one or the other or both.
- The enabler's report should be based on and fit with the evidence provided by the learner.

CHAPTER 8

Learning in a Multidisciplinary Setting

One of the newer truths for social work is that its contemporary position lies increasingly within multidisciplinary settings, relationships and combinations of service delivery. Practitioners in the field find themselves relating to statutory, private, voluntary and independent sector agencies and staff – as well as across the professional boundaries of education and health. A natural corollary of this ongoing and persistent development is that learning often takes place within these multidisciplinary constructs. This is an important factor to be borne in mind when delivering or receiving learning, and this chapter aims to explore some of the issues that stem from this development. How do we help learners understand their own professional background and culture without creating prejudice about other professions? Perhaps the first question to ask is – is multidisciplinary working a good idea? A typical response to the question would probably look something like this:

> All too often when people have complex needs spanning both health and social care good quality services are sacrificed for sterile arguments about boundaries. When this happens people, often the most vulnerable in our society … and those who care for them, find themselves in the no man's land between health and social services … it is poor organisation, poor practice, poor use of taxpayer's money – it is unacceptable. (DoH, 1998, p. 3)

And, of course, who would disagree with that? Looking in more detail multidisciplinary working offers much – increasing access for service users, strengthening of funding, promoting the strengths of specialism, avoiding duplication and offering, in some critiques: an appropriate response to the emerging complexity of the environment inhabited by social care.

But clearly, multidisciplinary working is not the simple, harmonious proposition suggested – as there are many sources of evidence that suggest an element of discord. Writers such as Glasby, for example, use the phrase 'Berlin Wall' when talking of the division between heath and social work (Glasby, 2003; Hudson et al., 1997). Indeed, Glasby concludes that for all the government's efforts to blur the boundaries between these groups, little is achieved, 'leaving the foundations well and truly in place' (Glasby, 2003, p. 975).

Glasby identifies five key areas where barriers are maintained:

1. *Structural* – where responsibility across agency boundaries leads to fragmentation, within and between sectors.
2. *Procedural* – differences in planning horizons, cycles, budget procedures, information systems, access and confidentiality protocols.
3. *Financial* – differences in funding mechanisms and bases; differences in stocks and flows of financial sources.
4. *Professional* – self interest, autonomy, competition for domains, competitive ideologies and values, job security, conflicts over clients interests and roles.
5. *Status and legitimacy* – organisational self interest/autonomy, domain competition and elected versus appointed agencies.

Whilst Glasby offers primarily structural and financial ways forward, (e.g. pooled budgets, integrated provision and lead commissioning) he fails to adequately deal with the professional issues he mentions, where the good intentions of 'joined up working' can break upon the rocks of professional culture and competition. To have a deeper, more critical understanding of some of these problems we need to understand not only professional boundaries but also professional cultures.

ACTIVITY

To begin to understand some aspects of professional culture, ask these questions of yourself and compare either with others directly, or from your knowledge of other professions.

Professional cultures – in a multidisciplinary setting, do the answers to the questions below differ between professional groups? If so why?

- Do users of the service call you by your first name?
- Do you call them by their first name?
- Would you accept a gift of food from a service user, such as a cake baked especially for you?
- Would your answer to that question be affected by your view of the cultural norms of that person?
- Would you accept an offer of a cup of tea or coffee in a service user's home?
- If invited to a social event, such as a wedding or party by a service user, how would you respond?

Source: adapted from Beale, 2005.

The expression of professional cultures around areas of direct contact with service users can be an illuminating introduction to their impact and extent. The issue of cultural differences between professionals has been identified as a key problem with multidisciplinary working for a number of years and we shall return to that theme later in this chapter. Social work, as we have noted, is in a challenging situation – not only in terms of its relationship to health services – but also to the broader social care arena. It appears that statutory social work, which for so long has characterised what social work 'is' must now awaken to a less dominant position:

> The profession of social work increasingly finds itself working in an extensive set of individualised, commercialised and fragmented services, within a mixed economy of care and set of often small and under funded community initiatives. Instead of enjoying a largely unquestioned hegemony in a field dominated by the local authority social services departments it is one of a range of occupational groups contributing to a diversity of provision. (Jordan, 2001, p. 533)

In terms of social work's professional culture this has also raised fundamental questions for *statutory* social work which finds itself not only locked within often uncomfortable relationships with other professions, but increasingly (desk) bound for a more distant relationship with the users of the services it provides. It is argued that the little community development social work is involved in

> signifies a vacuum, filled by the voluntary and community sectors, because public sector social work has become locked into a style of practice that is legalistic, formal, procedural and arms length and because office bound practitioners have largely lost touch with community networks as a result of this. (Jordan, 2001, p. 537)

It remains to be seen whether the spread of social work into the private, voluntary and independent sectors (as well as Health and Education) regains all or some of the profession's connection with the communities it serves. This brief analysis serves to indicate that the social work profession is undergoing change in many arenas and for many different reasons, but the context in which the profession approaches multidisciplinary working might not always be seen as positive. Perhaps what really matters is the pragmatic notion that multidisciplinary working is a reality of practice, it is with us to stay – and, indeed, there are good reasons for that to be so.

Of course, there are different levels of integration between agencies and disciplines – for example, a 'one stop shop' can house several professional groups – but do they all deliver separate services or are they 'joined up'? So, are we content to consider multidisciplinary and multi-professional working in the same way – where simply more than one discipline or profession is working together within a defined project? Whilst the simple answer is probably, yes – the more complex (and accurate) answer embraces the *complexity* of the situation. There are two axes to this: first, agencies, disciplines and professions are, of course different things. One agency, for example, can have within it different disciplines and different professional groups. One discipline can have within it a number of professional groups. The learner in such a setting needs to reflect on this dynamic. The second axis is that of the nature and level of connection between the component agencies, disciplines and professions – *how joined up are they?*

ACTIVITY

To understand the nature and extent of different agency and professional connections.

- Draw a spidergram of your view of the setting in which you work – try to encompass the different agencies, disciplines and professions within it.
- Consider the connections between the different groupings – do they connect in a structured way – or is there a reliance on personality?

Whilst the results of such an activity will obviously vary from setting to setting, the emergent complexity of the practitioner's networks should become evident. Approaching this from a critical perspective, we can begin to reflect on the strengths and weaknesses of such networks. What should we be looking for? How do we know whether we are looking at an effective way of multidisciplinary working? A range of literature exists on this issue, but it is interesting to briefly consider the view from the Treasury (HMSO) whose Public Service Productivity Panel (a group of senior business people and public sector managers) produced *Working Together: Effective Partnership Working on the Ground* in 2002. The group's conclusions are outlined below and it is interesting to view them through the eyes of a new learner in a multidisciplinary setting – in what ways, for example, is one able to see evidence of these factors in the learning setting?:

- *A balanced team* – with leaders, innovators and motivators.
- *Trust* – high levels are needed with confidence in collective decisions.
- *Motivation* – towards a common vision and new ways of working.
- *Conflict resolution mechanisms* – such as trading on a hierarchy of preferences.
- *Collaboration* – collective responsibility for decisions based on transparent, respectful discussion.
- *Clarity of objectives and responsibilities.*
- *Appropriate funding* – long-term funding for long-term issues which is easy to access.
- *Room for manoeuvre* – especially in flexible use of budgets.

Enablers, in their work with learners may find it useful to pare down the volume of factors and actors and look at one or more aspects in particular. How, for example are the elements of trust and collaboration being applied to multidisciplinary learning, how often do different disciplines actually sit down and learn together? The problem can often be the difficulties in getting professions to actually sit 'side by side'. Having gained that considerable achievement, other problems can emerge. Pollard looked at the experience of several hundred nurses and social work students (Pollard et al., 2004). They found that most students were favourably inclined towards inter-professional *learning* but negative about inter-professional *interaction*. Interestingly for the social work profession, mature and experienced respondents were more likely to be negative about inter-professional interaction in general. Social work and occupational therapist students were found to be the least inclined to work inter-professionally. What does this tell us about the social work profession, its relation to others and the role of enablers in such networks?

One cannot underestimate the strength of the differences between professions and disciplines. One reason for this may be that different professions have different cultures – but for many these cultures are part of who we are as people. Considering the literature on the links between profession and identity, we can explore the connection between who we are as a person and who we are as a professional worker. Much of the material in this area begins with a focus on the notion of professional socialisation – how, usually through professional training, we learn to become a professional worker. This has also been termed 'enculturation' – whereby we learn the norms, value and roles associated with the profession (Rynanen, 2001; Olesen and Whittaker, 1970). Greenwood was one of the first writers to analyse social work from this perspective, when he looked at the pervasiveness of the professional role in other (personal) areas of the workers lives, 'the work life invades the after work life and the sharp demarcation between the work hours and the leisure hours disappears. The professional is a person whose work becomes his life' (Greenwood, 1957, p. 15).

Any hard-working professional reading this definition will surely see an aspect of truth within these thoughts – how often do we take our work home? Socialise with colleagues? Talk and think about work? Thus, for Greenwood, because of such things as our sense of vocation, our commitment to our professional task and our value base, the boundary between who we are at work and who we are at home becomes blurred.

This understanding enhances the sense of what it means to be a professional and also goes some way to explain what makes it difficult to work with other professions where differences are more than phrases in policies and procedures – they are differences in identities. This, in turn, directs our attention to the creation of these identities – they don't simply descend upon the professional worker, they are, at least to some extent, learned. Indeed, one might readily argue that professional training is where this identity is created – where *we learnt to be who we are*. Take, for example, Merton, writing in 1957 on medical schools:

> It is their function to transmit the culture of medicine and to advance that culture … and to provide him (sic) with a professional identity so that he comes to think, act and feel like a physician. It is their problem to enable the medical man to live up to the expectations of the professional role long after he has left the sustaining value-environment provided by the medical school. (Merton, Reader and Kendall, 1957, p. 4)

Merton underlines the impact of professional learning at the training stage in terms of knowledge, behaviour and culture. Here we get a firm sense of the longevity envisaged for these 'implants' – they are designed to last a professional lifetime. However, we all know that this is not as static as is suggested – the shifts and eddies in what is deemed important as professional knowledge (witness the growth of SCIE in recent years) shows us that the situation is not static but *emergent*, developing and dynamic. Hughes importantly notes that there are a whole range of processes attached to professional education that are designed to keep the professional culture alive, 'through time and generations … by which it is added to by learning and teaching' (Hughes, 1984, p. 399). We can think of practice learning as key to this notion of carrying on the professional torch.

Yet, this is not a simple process – reflect on the changes to social work education over the last 20 years. The political situation of the profession can also impact on its sense of self. Statutory social work in England, for example, is firmly located within Social Service Departments which themselves are located within the structures of Local Authorities and beyond through government. The social work profession is thus most commonly situated within powerful organisational structures that inevitably impact on professional knowledge and arguably, professional self. But even this scenario is changing – as we have considered earlier – with social work's new emerging relationship with the private, voluntary and independent sectors around the delivery of social care. As social work's relationships with a range of other agencies become more complex, one may perceive the dangers of a 'porous' effect – the seeping in of contrasting knowledge, culture, values and ways of working. Some post-modern views emphasise the fluidity of identities, where they become more complex, more confusing and *fragmented*. Thus, just as race is no longer simply a consideration of black or white, but is mediated by our conceptions of age, class, gender and more detailed conceptions of ethnicity – so professional identity becomes mediated by a range of policy developments, structures and relationships (Wilding, 2000). Other authors have considered the similar development of '*fractured identities*' (Bradley, 2002, p. 480). Of course, policy and general central control of agendas will attempt to direct this growing complexity (of profession and organisation) and it may be that what we have in terms of our identities and our structures doesn't fit the (post) modern world:

> The old institutions have been defined as wanting. That search for solutions, for new systems and structures, in a more plural messier world will continue. The risk of course – and it could be gain for central government – is a bewildering cacophony of ad hocery in which … no one quite knows who, if anyone, is responsible for what. (Wilding, 2000, p. 8)

These shifting professional relationships will inevitably result in reflections on the nature of our professional role and the control we have over it. Given the context of this analysis, we should never underestimate the power of professional difference which, as we have discussed, becomes bound together with our sense of *who we are* and *what we became* through our learning as a trainee. This then becomes our premise for learning in a multidisciplinary setting – the enhancement of an understanding of the importance of professional identity. From that point we can see some of the difficulties in learning side by side:

> Shared learning can only take place when sharing is possible, that is, when individuals or professional groups are willing to 'let go' of their own knowledge and expertise and allow others to use it. The failure of consolidation on any scale may well be due as much as lack of readiness and ability of professions to 'share' as to any other barrier. (Low and Weinstein, 2000, p. 207)

For Low and Weinstein, the conclusion is to focus on inter-professional *learning* for collaborative practice rather than inter-professional *education*, understanding that such learning cannot guarantee collaborative practice but can certainly enhance the skills needed to perform effectively in these settings. They rightly also underline the need to ensure that an emphasis is placed on field-based education and service user involvement. The learner and enabler must work to understand their professional identity in relation to others and make explicit their awareness of the particular skills they deploy in their daily professional conduct.

ACTIVITY

To construct explicit statements about identities and boundaries within an experience of inter-professional working and reflect on their validity.

Taking Payne's suggestion, we need to '*make an issue*' and '*think explicitly about*' the following:

- The identity that agencies, professions and disciplines have for different participants.
- The boundaries between agencies, professions and disciplines.
- The resources used and which agencies, professions and disciplines they are.
- The skills needed to work in collaborative settings.

Take these topics into discussion between learner and enabler; try to delve into differences between worker perceptions and organisational perceptions of boundaries.

Source: drawn from Adams, Dominelli and Payne (2002, p. 257).

This activity should help us to move from assumptions and inference to more concrete statements about the reality of multidisciplinary working. But how can we gain access to some of these issues? One starting point might be to think explicitly about the creation of our own professional identity – why did we come into the profession, why did we elect to practice in the way we do and why did we choose to become enablers? Furthermore, given the central role that enablers have in the transmission of professional identity – how do we actually do that? Another, less introspective starting point is an understanding of the 'professional body'. It might be interesting to follow through some key websites that offer mission statements, codes of practice and so on. Similarly, annual reports and organisational documents often present a particular picture of an agency – beyond a diagram of its structure. Content analysis of items such as mission statements can be a way of shining some of the dullness off what can be dreary documents. In this method the learner and enabler can decide to gather two or more mission statements and can, prior to their collection, play 'bingo' with words that they anticipate will be located within the statements. This can draw out key, shared words that may point towards shared professional languages – for all the differences there will always be many similarities. On a more personal and more expressive level one might envisage working side by side with a colleague from another discipline. Perhaps it is only by exploring, talking and engaging with others that we can fully understand the nature of their differences and, in this sense, multidisciplinary learning encompasses much of our understanding of anti-oppressive practice. There are *cultural* differences between organisations that may well be unearthed. Some of these differences may be based on prejudice, misunderstanding or sheer lack of information. The obvious point is that learners in a multidisciplinary setting have an obligation to ensure that they learn about the network of organisational relationships in which they are engaged. But, an important step is also an understanding of our own attitudes as learners and enablers, and our different work ethics. Social workers, like everyone else can possess stereotypical images of others. If we think briefly of the images we come across in the media, what would a 'typical' doctor, youth worker, teacher, police office and health visitor look like? What do we discover? Probably that the images we have of other professionals, as well as ourselves, are the products of our experience, values, training and so forth – but that our experiences are unlikely to reveal any objective truth. One only has to reflect for the briefest of moments on the tabloid view of social workers to realise the strength and pervasiveness of these images. Of course, such images affect multidisciplinary working – and what is expected of us as social workers. Social workers do not operate in isolation. Their work brings them into contact with a range of agencies, professions, disciplines and, of course, other social workers. Looking outside the profession we can see that each of these groups is able to exert some influence on the expectations of what social workers do and how they do it.

ACTIVITY

To reflect on who expects what of social workers and how social workers may handle conflicting expectations.

Stage A
On a piece of paper, construct a series of boxes and give each a heading that represents different members of the social worker's role set – nurse, youth worker, police officer, teacher, doctor, service user, courts and so forth. Each grouping or organisation will have its own views on what the social worker's task is about. Use the blank space in each box to jot down a concise phrase or key words that typify what you perceive these expectations to be.

Nurse	Youth worker	Police officer	Teacher	Doctor

Stage B
Having completed the boxes, examine them to identify which sets of boxes contain

- similar or identical expectations,
- differing expectations but which are potentially compatible with each other, and
- contradictory or conflicting expectations.

It is this last grouping that will be likely to pose problems for the social worker. Issues raised by this are the focus of

Stage C
Where the box contents are contradictory (and in particular where there is conflict in your own box) think about the following.

- Why does this conflict arise?
- Is this conflict inevitable?
- Are there ways of avoiding it? Or minimising it?
- If not, in what ways do you/might you cope with it?

To move forward from this acknowledgement of difference we can begin to make some assessment of the nature of the organisational cultures that we inhabit – and how they might compare with the culture of other organisational structures within, for example, Health and Education. Salaman (1995), in his influential work on management, suggests that we explore the culture of an organisation by looking at varying aspects of its 'orientation':

- *Affective orientation* (how bound up with each other do people become in the work setting?)
- *Orientation towards causality* (i.e. is responsibility for problems attributed to people or to the system?)
- *Hierarchical orientation* (how do people respond to differences in position, power and responsibility?)
- *Change orientation* (how far are people willing to embark on new ventures?)
- *Individual/collectivist orientation* (how far do people choose to work alone or with others?)
- *Unitary/pluralist orientation* (how do people in different interest groups relate to each other?

This typology can be very informative as a tool for analysis. If we briefly consider change orientation, for example, the learner and enabler can begin to reflect on their perceptions of the organisation they inhabit in regard to change. Where does change come from (top-down, bottom-up?) How is change viewed by staff? ('nothing new under the sun'), Is there any connection between learning and change in the organisation? Do different professional groups, different hierarchical roles have different views on change? The complex task for the learner (and enabler) in such settings is to develop their understandings of different cultures – whilst not forgetting who they are and what their professional role in relation to others actually means for their development and learning.

Using the Expertise of Others

Having established an understanding of the complexity of multi-professional, multidisciplinary learning we should spend some time reflecting on models for the appropriate involvement of others in learning and enabling in such complex settings where social workers are present. For the enabler, there is the obvious requirement that the team, in its broadest sense, should have ownership of the learner. There may be a significant amount of groundwork in producing a plan for how learners, from any professional background can best learn within the team. It is vital that the enabler puts effort into this well in advance of the arrival of the leaner and constructs arrangements with colleagues across the professional boundaries. The outcome from this discussion should be the creation of a shared understanding of expertise in the team – which learners can freely tap into. Thus, for example, in a Youth Offending Team (YOT) the new learner might, as an aspect of induction, benefit from planned sessions with members of staff on specific topics, for example, the probation officer discussing pre-sentence reports, the police officer discussing the criminal law and so forth.

Rather more complex is the involvement of others in the assessment of learners. The simplest models locate the enabler as the central feedback figure who has the clear, final responsibility for the assessment of the learner. In such a model the enabler can become a hub which all those involved in providing learning opportunities for the learner can feed into. This model shouldn't become stretched even where an off-site enabler, perhaps not a specialist in the learning setting, has to make assessment decisions. The off-site should simply ensure that whilst retaining their formal assessment role, they pay due regard to feedback from the work-based supervisor or colleague from another profession. As long as learners, enablers and others involved are all clear, this model should hold up well in multidisciplinary settings.

Mantell (1998) is one of the relatively few researchers into the area of multiprofessional learning and talks of the importance of the (student) learner feeling 'contained' in its most positive sense – with clear support, clear boundaries and permission to explore feelings engendered by their learning. Strong pre-placement planning can avoid a feeling of being 'overwhelmed' – perhaps combined with relatively more time spent with the learner in the first week. Mantell also found that learners wanted to feel part of the team they newly inhabited, valuing opportunities for shadowing and being shown examples from others' workloads. He promotes the notion of explicitly addressing issues of status and power, even salaries, because of the dialogue it creates and its relation to wider power differences in society (Mantell, 1998). Thus, whist the complexity of the environment makes it feel as though learning takes place on 'shifting sands', Mantell is in no doubt about the benefits of well-organised learning opportunities in such settings:

> Students placed in multidisciplinary settings are in a prime position to break down cultural stereotypes, gain an understanding of other

disciplines, and work together to provide a coherent service to the client. The concepts of role and status help us to understand the complexity of this process and the challenges that the student might face. (Mantell, 1998, p. 181)

Parker (2004) talks of the usefulness of 'learning sets' in multidisciplinary settings. Learners from a range of disciplines can form learning *alliances* around specific topics or practice related areas. Different approaches to issues of theory and practice can safely be explored in such supportive environments which may benefit from being 'outside' of supervisory assessment. We can take this notion a step further and, if we have our multidisciplinary learning sets, begin to develop them with the idea of 'problem based learning' (PBL) (see, for example, Taylor, 1997; Baldwin and Burgess, 1992). PBL was actually developed in medicine and engineering fields and, at its simplest, involves the formation of a group using problems or scenarios as a basis for study. Existing knowledge and learning is shared and the (usually facilitated) group identifies what it then needs to know and how it is going to find it out, drawing on a wide range of resources. The group reconvenes to discuss progress, share learning, evaluate and contemplate next steps. Clearly this model, whilst not requiring multidisciplinary teams, benefits enormously from such a construct – effectively modelling a learning, multiprofessional grouping.

For all our efforts in understanding differences within a multidisciplinary team, the importance of communication and the need for reflection on our own views, we can only conclude that these are complex settings that we must respond to in imaginative, creative and fundamentally *critical* ways. If, as learners and enablers, we engage with multidisciplinary settings in a way that embraces their complexity and fragmented nature, we are more likely to understand our experience. One must therefore develop ways of learning and enabling that can enhance (*make explicit*) critical understanding. We will now explore the notion of the practitioner-researcher as one possible answer to this challenge.

The Practitioner-researcher

The starting point for this line of thought is that learners and enablers working in (or seeking to understand) a multidisciplinary setting must develop their research awareness. They must explore the research literature that exists in relation to their setting but, equally importantly, develop their own skills as researchers to enable their critical research upon their multidisciplinary working and practice. In this sense the researcher and practitioner are the same person. The literature surrounding inter-professional working and learning is surprisingly unable to provide a reassuring evidence base for its effectiveness. Indeed, some authors believe that there is little convincing evidence that inter-professional learning will promote team work, better collaboration or better service user outcomes; likening the search for such evidence to the quest for the 'holy grail' (Mattick and Bligh, 2006). However, surely we must agree with these authors that the only conclusion to be reached is that the evidence must be found by well-designed and rigorous research. We would further add that social work is perhaps the ideal profession to act as a catalyst for such endeavour, agreeing that, 'arguably social work is *the* joined up profession – (seeking) to liaise, to mediate and to negotiate' (Frost et al., 2005, p. 196).

It could be argued that practitioners also need to develop their own research skills because of the failings of traditional models of academic research. Cheetham et al. (1992), in a study of social work effectiveness, for example, wrote several studies looking at a whole plethora of methodologies, but significant by its absence is the voice of the practitioner, the deliverer of service. There are surprisingly (and depressingly) few accounts of practice by practitioners. Social work practice, it would seem, has become a thing described (and evaluated) by people other than those who actually do it. Whilst the literature in this field is limited, particularly on the research relationship between higher education and social work, there are some interesting parallel discussions and reflections within social work education, notably Eraut (1994), Rowlings (2000) and Henkel (1995). Eraut (1994), for example, believes that in any form of professional education there will be tensions between it and its university base. Rowlings (2000), argues that social work education's relationship to the two 'constituencies' of social work and higher education are characterised by distance rather than integration and notes the growing distrust within the social work profession of academia. Rowlings argues that managerialism creates a fear of risk taking and thus compliance to guidelines and procedures is highly regarded. This, she suggests, creates a climate where the use of imagination and a questioning of established ways of working is frowned upon and discouraged. However, whilst Rowlings is concerned that professional development takes its focus as the *workplace*, for McLeod this is an opportunity to be seized – the chance to redraw these traditional, hierarchical relationships. McLeod demands that practitioners seek to 'turn around the relationship between practitioners and academics, so that academics become consultants and resource providers but practitioners remain in control of their process of personal inquiry' (McLeod, 1999, p. 20).

McLeod points towards a significant conclusion – practitioners need to develop their 'knowledge skills (and) take more responsibility for the knowledge base of their profession' – to best engage in the 'reconstruction of practice' (McLeod, 1999, p. 204). Eraut strikes a similar chord when urging professional workers to develop their 'disposition to theorise' and 'bring their knowledge under critical control' (Eraut, 1994, pp. 71, 90). Learners must develop the skills to become more active in creating and developing their own knowledge base in their multidisciplinary work by becoming practitioner-researchers. Enablers should develop their research expertise and allow their knowledge to become an aspect of the learning process. Enablers should be a key part of the development of practitioner-researchers. But this is not an easy task because such skills and ambitions in practice appear to have been lost if, indeed, they were ever present. Research and evaluation, 'have tended to be little-used terms in the vocabulary of social workers' (McIvor, 1996, p. 209).

Cheetham argues that there is an ethical and professional obligation on workers to provide help in its most effective form (Cheetham, 1992). How can this be done in a multidisciplinary setting if the practitioners – the ones active in the work setting, are not evaluating that help? We would also argue that whilst the practitioner-researcher is important they cannot and should not exist outside a close relationship with academic research. Rowlings argues for higher education's, 'culture of dispute, debate and exploration of the alternative' (Rowlings, 2000, p. 49). The academic community can provide the profession (and the multidisciplinary team) with methodological robustness, support on ethically principled research and, perhaps more importantly, a powerful allied voice. Yet, there is a sense that the current lines of connection need to be redrawn. McCrystal and Godfrey's illuminating insight on this very topic argues vehemently for a greater sense of partnership and offers seven key fundamental principles that may best serve what they term, practitioner-researcher partnerships:

- Recognition of the strengths of the partner's professional experience which they bring to joint working.
- Delegation of roles and responsibilities based on this mutual recognition
- Mutual acceptance of the relevant strengths of each partner at a personal as well as professional level.
- Negotiations based on a commitment to a common goal.
- Working both jointly and independently when appropriate to achieve common goals.
- The development of a professional rapport that bridges the professional divide; and,
- formalising all aspects of the collaborative work in order to obtain in an efficient way the mutual benefits for both members of the partnership. (McCrystal and Godfrey, 2001, p. 548)

McCrystal and Godfrey offer a way forward for the development of a new partnership between researcher in practice and researchers in education. If an effective partnership can be drawn up, both profession and academic institution can potentially benefit. How similar McCrystal and Godfrey's notions of partnership are to those from the Treasury and Home Office are considered earlier in relation to effective multidisciplinary working. It could be argued that we need to think in the broadest of terms when we think of multidisciplinary working – a range of professional approaches, including those brought to the table by academia, in the construction of an emergent knowledge base for multidisciplinary working.

The development of a practitioner-research aspect to the learner role has obvious links to the parallel development of knowledge skills in the profession, but links can also be made to issues of autonomy and culture. For example, the practitioner-researcher led development of a knowledge base for an emergent process of multidisciplinary work might better reflect the culture and ethos of the contributing professions and allow for a greater degree of control, by the profession, in the day-to-day work of practitioners. Learners and enablers are, by their very definition, ideally placed to develop their research skills within multidisciplinary settings – who else, on such a regular basis reflects on and evaluates practice so closely?

Learners and enablers alike would do well to reflect on the use of research in their current setting but, in any event, attention must be paid by both to the evaluation of practice. Evaluation, in this context, is simply the assessment of the effectiveness of a given intervention. The integration of research mindedness in the evaluation of everyday practice is one of the cornerstones of developing the practitioner-researcher. Learners and enablers should be clear about what they are trying to achieve, how interventions are progressing, reflecting on outcomes and adapting their approach in the light of their findings. This book is not a guide to that process but rather offers some simple indicators of how practice might be evaluated. The complexity of the multitude of interventions and the settings in which they take place means that no one model of practice evaluation is generically applicable, but the Preston-Shoot and Williams model gently brokers the notion for learners of what needs to be engaged with in the evaluation of practice – its importance should reflect the importance placed on research generally in the setting.

ACTIVITY

To engage with introductory notions of the evaluation of practice.

Follow (or adapt) this model to the evaluation of practice:

1. Describe the current situation as precisely as possible.
2. Describe the broad aim or desired outcome of work.
3. Identify feasible objectives and specific goals; the achievement of which will help to accomplish the desired outcome.
4. Decide and describe carefully the intervention designed to achieved the desired situation, including the methods and resources required.
5. Identify indicators which will reveal change.
6. Decide who will record what and how.
7. Set out step 1 to step 6 as a plan for evaluating the effect of the work and implement it.
8. Establish and review the results of the intervention prior to either a return to step 1 or termination and subsequent follow-up.

Source: adapted from Preston-Shoot and Williams, 1995.

This activity can provide illustrations of effective practice and can be easily applied to different arenas of joint working. Readers interested in developing research skills might consider Shaw (1999).

Critical Learning in Multidisciplinary Settings

As useful as the development of such skills is, we must also reflect on how often, as practitioners, we are engaged in such evaluation. Learners and enablers might also reflect on the nature of the above model and its suitability for social work practice evaluation. Thus, for example, does it allow sufficient space to hear the service user's voice? Is it generally too positivist a tool, relying too heavily on quantitative notions rather than qualitative outcomes – does the service user feel better as a result? And anyway, who are Preston-Shoot and Williams! The point being raised is that this research tool – *like every single other research tool produced* – should be exposed to critical scrutiny. The work of the Critical Appraisal Skills Programme (CASP) focuses on this very issue, providing, in effect, tools for the scrutiny of research projects in health and social care (see http://www.phru.nhs.uk/casp) – and, of course, that tool itself should be scrutinised.

The concept of the practitioner-researcher, of itself, is enhanced when combined with that of the critical practitioner. In essence critical practice is *questioning* practice – where we question our work as practitioners, the structures in which we work and our methods of intervention. Critical practice is a form of professional behaviour that seeks to get under the skin of the apparent reality to achieve a better grasp of practice. Critical practice 'enables us to assess situations so as to make structural connections that penetrate the surface of what we encounter and locate what is apparent within wider contexts' (Adams et al., 2002, p. xxi).

Clearly, from our discussions about practitioner-researchers, there are many links here. Indeed it has been argued that being critical inherently requires us to act like a critical researcher (Harvey, 1990). Other authors, such as Fook have developed and extended the concept of critical practice into a broader critical *approach* which more fully reflects the needs of the learner and enabler in a multidisciplinary setting and more explicitly develops the political nature of the structural context. Fook summarises her view of the basic elements of a critical approach as the following.

- A commitment to a structural analysis of social and personally experienced problems, that is, an understanding of how personal problems might be traced to socio-economic structures, and that the 'personal' and 'political' realms are inextricably linked.
- A commitment to emancipatory forms of analysis and action (incorporating both anti-oppressive and anti-exploitative stances).
- A stance of social critique (including an acknowledgement and critique of the social control functions of the social work profession and the welfare system).
- A commitment to social change. (Fook, 2002, p. 5)

These commitments surely find some resonance in the political and value base of the social work profession. It must, therefore, be important that learners and enablers extend these critical notions into their approach to the multidisciplinary setting.

We have looked extensively at the complexities of learning for the social worker in a multi-professional environment and hopefully have found some sources of opportunities for enhancing learning given the demands of the setting. The difficulties of effective multidisciplinary working and learning have not been brushed past in this chapter – it is a difficult state to achieve, but, as we argued right at the beginning, there are some senses in which its logic is impregnable. It is a desirable aim. Yet, the tensions located in these settings are not sterile; rather they are linked to our professional self and as such must not be underestimated. The learner placing their feet on these shifting sands needs all the support an enabler can offer. Enablers need to draw what support they can from like-minded colleagues and expressions of the learning organisation that exist within the workplace. Nevertheless, for all these doubts, concerns and worries, social work's relationships with other disciplines in the field will, most often, be with colleagues who also want to develop strong effective services for users of services – whose interests we all have at heart. There is, most likely, a sense of shared vision and broadly shared values and this last exercise is designed to create the interesting environment of a 'what if'. In this case, how interesting it will be for learners and enablers alike, perhaps from a range of professional groupings, to come together and imagine that they have sat down, for the very first time and asked the question, what if?

ACTIVITY

To facilitate 'blue skies' thinking about the construction of new forms of multidisciplinary working

Effective ways of working together

- Organise into small groups – of not more than four.
- Agree that you each represent an agency/type of agency, with which you are familiar – so that you have around three to four 'agencies'.
- Imagine a new, shared service that you might provide.
- Imagine five barriers to (your) partnership working and then discuss ways to overcome them.
- Agree an agenda for the first meeting of the partnership including a 'visioning' process – how will this be facilitated?
- What success factors do you envisage in this partnership?

Key Learning Points

- Partnership is an increasingly important aspect of social work practice, but it is not without its problems. Professional identities can become fractured in certain circumstances and there can be an unwillingness to share learning across professional boundaries. Multidisciplinary working is not effective in itself.
- Inter-professional learning is important, as is understanding the different cultures and identities of different professional groups. Workers in these settings need to develop an approach that ensures service users receive a better service – based on research of their environment.
- Enablers can use notions of the 'researcher practitioner' and 'critical practice' to develop the learner best suited to working in multidisciplinary settings.

CHAPTER 9

Dealing with Difficulties

Despite the best-laid plans difficulties do occur in work-based learning. It would be tempting to say that if people followed the guidelines offered in the previous chapters then difficulties would be kept to a minimum, but they can, and do arise from a range of areas. This chapter attempts to categorise some of the sorts of difficulties that occur. The first section of this chapter deals with reasons why difficulties arise and makes some suggestions about how to deal with them. In the 'people business' inevitably categories are never clear-cut but overlap, so the reader should bear this in mind. The second section of the chapter considers the process of dealing with a learner who is not yet competent.

When things go wrong it is tempting to look for a scapegoat. For the enabler this may be blaming the learner or the educational programme for not preparing the learner appropriately. For the learner it may be blaming the enabler or the educational programme or even the service user. Difficulties are inevitable but they do not necessarily always lead to breakdown and failure. Early recognition and acknowledgement of difficulties by all parties involved in the learning process is important, as is a commitment by all involved to attempt to overcome the difficulties. Hoping that difficulties will somehow resolve themselves is tempting as working through them can cause a great deal of soul searching, but it is rarely a successful strategy. Difficulties when resolved appropriately can be 'ego strengthening'. Those left to fester may even cause greater problems later, which can lead to breakdown and failure having far-reaching effects on all concerned.

The enabler and learners need to remember that they are not alone when dealing with difficulties. The social work education programme on which the learner is enrolled will have a commitment to supporting the learner and trying to resolve any difficulties which occur. Staff on these programmes generally have come across common problems in work-based learning before. Although there will generally be a named tutor attached to the learner they will have access to a wealth of experience within the staff team. Enablers or learners should contact the named person for support with difficulties which may arise.

Difficulties within the Learning Partnership

Differences of expectations and perception

Two or more people enter the learning relationship with different views or different nuances on the same view. If these views are not expressed, communication difficulties may ensue. For example, enablers may consider that their role is to do everything possible to ensure that learners are successful in their learning. Success would be measured by the demonstration of competence and providing quality service to service users. They see themselves as helpful and 'rooting' for the learner. They would probably want to know of any difficulties that the learner experiences in order to help iron them out. However the learner may see the enabler as someone who is there to check on their competence and thus someone to be wary of, someone who always needs the right response, someone to avoid discussing difficulties with incase this influences their assessment. They do not necessarily see the enabler as someone who is there to help. Unless each party within the relationship is explicit about how it sees its role and that of the other party, differences can go unacknowledged. All behaviour by one party will then be viewed through the preconceived ideas of the other. Thus on the one hand innocent questions on the part of the enabler about how the learner is getting on can be viewed as gathering evidence for a judgement about competence. Enablers on the other hand may come to conclusions about a learner's motivation from questions that they ask when setting up the learning experience. Students are often preoccupied with the practicalities of undertaking practice learning in a setting which may be a distance from their home and require adjustments in their personal and working life. Questions such as 'What time can I finish?' may be interpreted by the enabler as a lack of commitment and not as anxieties about juggling caring responsibilities alongside practice opportunities. Obviously some of these initial views will be sorted out with further discussion but it does require both parties to keep open minds and be aware of their own preconceived ideas and prejudices at a time of possible heightened anxiety.

Most people can easily accept that learners will feel anxious when starting a practice learning opportunity as they have to get to grips with new people, new practices, a new organisational culture and structures as well as prove their competence in key roles. Learners who are being encouraged to develop new skills in their existing work place will not have the anxieties about new cultures and people, but may have feelings about becoming de-skilled when attempting new areas of work. They may worry that if they do not succeed in their new area of learning, this may have repercussions on their status as a worker. Less common is seeing the possible anxieties which the enabler may be experiencing. Comments inadvertently made by university tutors have been known to utterly throw enablers into a state of panic about their ability to help the learner learn anything. For example, 'this is a really good student with an excellent grasp of theory' or 'this one will keep you on your toes, they never accept anything without a challenge'. First time enablers may well be wondering whether or not they are up to the role. Other enablers may have seen colleagues experience difficulties with certain learners and wonder whether or not they will suffer the same fate. As people who regularly teach new enablers we see their anxieties in stark relief but find learners are less accepting of the fact that the enabler can be as anxious as they are. Thus misunderstandings about the way the 'other' is feeling in the relationship can lead to relationships floundering in the early days of the practice. First impressions are after all quite difficult to dispel and can colour all future interactions.

Cowburn argues that the competence model of assessment involves positivist methods and 'considers that the assessor is effectively an intellect, divorced from identity, race, gender, class, culture, who can provide a "value-free" assessment of the student's performance' (Cowburn et al., 2000, p. 631).

They go on to say that learner and enabler are also required to underpin their practice with anti-oppressive practice principles both in their work with each other and with service users. They consider that this tension can generally be accommodated within the learning relationship until the issue of marginality or failure rears its ugly head. In these circumstances there is a tendency for the positivist paradigm to assert itself and by tacit agreement the more experienced worker in this situation, the enabler, is seen as right. Little acknowledgement is given to the assumptions which underlie the process of assessment. The enabler is seen as neutral and value-free. This idea comes from the scientific method, which tends to consider objects of study from the standpoint of the dominant group. The model of the enabler as the objective assessor is dominant in the competency-based assessment system. Yet an anti-oppressive practice stance would acknowledge that there are several perspectives to consider in any interaction between people and that there is a difference in the power each has which affects whose definition becomes accepted. It is the surfacing of these perspectives and negotiation between them, which leads to a more rounded assessment in keeping with anti-oppressive practice.

Clearly preparation and discussion early in the practice learning opportunity are important to try and prevent misunderstandings. If communication seems to be difficult it might well be useful to employ techniques from social work practice such as 'tuning in' to the other person or 'reframing' our own views to help see another side of the situation. This, of course, needs checking out with the other party but these techniques can sometimes unlock communication difficulties.

The role of enabler carries with it a great deal of power. Enablers have expert power knowledge of the agency and their experience. Legitimate power comes from the role, which gives them the power to pass or fail, to facilitate or not. Learners can feel overwhelmed and powerless in their situation particularly if the enabler is from a group within society which is seen as powerful. This is exacerbated if the learner comes from a group seen by society as less powerful. The enabler cannot negate the enabler's power but they can use it positively. This requires the source of the enabler's power to be made explicit and the way it is used to be legitimate, consistent and clear (Morrison, 2000).

In order to deal with the difficulties highlighted, enablers should check out whether or not they have considered and included the learner's viewpoint on issues. They should address the learner's previous experiences of learning and being supervised so that they understand their perception of the experiences they are about to embark upon. They should also make explicit their view of their role and ask for the learner's view of the enabler's role to check out any differences. Danbury and Sharpe (1999) have developed a series of exercises to facilitate this task. They ask both learners and enablers to place their answers to a series of questions along a continuum. For example, on direct observation they ask practice teachers to locate their answer on the continuum:

1. I expect to directly observe the student's practice with service users

1	2	3	4	5

Minimal number required   Most of the time

2. I expect to observe the student's practice directly

1	2	3	4	5

Early in placement   At the end

3. I expect students to participate in direct observation

1	2	3	4	5

Enthusiastically   Reluctantly

4. I regard direct observation to be an assessment method, which is

1	2	3	4	5

Very useful   Not useful

5. I regard that as a teaching method, direct observation is

1	2	3	4	5

Very useful   Not useful

One of the things I like about this method is

One of the things I dislike about this method is

When involved in direct observation things I expect students to consider are:

Source: Sharpe and Danbury (1999, pp. 58–59).

The student is then asked the same questions from his or her point of view. Once learners and enablers have both completed the questions they exchange the answers and consider direct observation from the point of view of the other. This will surface differences. It does, of course, depend on both parties being honest and the learners being prepared to offer answers that they might think are 'wrong'. If this is to work both parties must be willing to accept the views of the other. This sort of questionnaire can be used in relation to other areas of the learning relationship, for example, around general expectations about how a learner and enabler relate to each other or expectations about supervision.

Once acknowledged differences can be continually discussed, and hopefully this will allow each participant to understand the other's views more clearly and misunderstandings will be less likely. Where possible, compromises can be made which would suit all parties. There will be, however, some 'given' requirements which are set by either the educational programme or the social work agency. Discussion about why these are set may help acceptance. If differences are not acknowledged, and the relationship is not trusting and honest it can impact on the learners' ability to learn. Mediating in situations of stalemate may well be the role of the university tutor who may be able to encourage both parties to recognise the views of the other.

Differences of opinion about competence

Difficulties can arise within the learning partnership when there are differences of opinion between the learner and the enabler about the learner's progress or lack of progress. Social work is an area that does not have cut and dried responses to people's difficulties. Differences of opinion about the way forward in any one situation abound. It is likely therefore that there may well be differences of opinion about a learner's progress and whether it is sufficient to demonstrate competence (see Chapter 7 on Assessment for further discussion on this area). In order to avoid stalemate and polarisation of opinions it is necessary for enablers to seek evidence for their assessment from a range of sources. It is useful if others can also view these sources, for example, case records, reports, letters or even videos of practice. This will allow the enabler to gain a range of views. Similarly to prevent bias it is useful

for the learner to be seen in practice by other practitioners and for the
views of the service user/s and carers to be sought about the practice
of the learner. All these sources of evidence need to be weighed against
one another and where they are in conflict a balanced judgement be
made. Learners whose views on their own competence differ markedly
from the views of several other people may need help accepting this
and may allege collusion between the people who have been assessing
them. When drawing up the learning agreement some thought should
be given to how differences of opinion are going to be resolved. This is
now the time to instigate this procedure and remind all involved that
when they were drawing up the agreement and before views became
polarised this procedure was agreed upon. If any party feels the procedure is not robust enough a third party may need to be drawn in to
negotiate an alternative. The other aspect to this area of difficulty is
that learners may not have actually done something wrong, that is they
are not seen to be incompetent, but they have not demonstrated competence. They may ask for evidence of what they have done wrong and
this would not be available. Their claim could be that they did not
know what was expected of them in certain situations. Clearly this is
difficult to retrieve when it has happened so making clear what is
expected of learners at the outset may prevent this. We have stressed in
other places that it is important for learners and enablers to discuss key
roles and their interpretation. This should help misunderstandings
occurring about what is expected. Some educational programmes have
in the past identified both positive and negative indicators of competence based on the work by Thompson, Osada and Anderson (1994).
This may be a useful exercise to undertake to ensure that both parties
have similar understandings, although it can take considerable time. If
disagreements cannot be resolved the university will have systems to
review evidence and may in some circumstances instigate a full review of
the learning opportunities and the learner's work through a third party.

Unhelpful processes in supervision

Mention has already been made of the games which can be played in
supervision in the Chapter 5 on Supervision. As we have already highlighted the importance of anxiety in the learning relationship, it would
be useful here to explain how anxiety could produce defence mechanisms in both the learner and the enabler. These can have an adverse

impact on the effectiveness of both (Morrison, 2002). When more things seem to be going on under the supervision table rather than across the top, it is time to consider defence mechanisms. These are ways of unconsciously avoiding feelings. Feelings are an integral part of 'people work' but are often neglected and can make people uncomfortable. If they are addressed, this is often done in a superficial manner. Feelings can either push someone into doing something or get in the way of their functioning (Thompson, 2002). Some agencies or groups of staff within an agency have cultures that negate the influence of feelings. It is seen as 'soft' to admit that the impact of the feelings arising from the work is in turn affecting the workers' functioning. Morrison (2002) describes the main defence mechanisms in the following list.

- Splitting occurs when we divide what we consider to be our good feelings from our bad feelings because we cannot cope with the tensions between the two. This may result in denial of some feelings or excessive feelings of despair and paranoia.
- Projection occurs when parts of self, which are difficult to acknowledge, are projected onto another person. An example would be of a learner projecting competence onto the enabler, which means they then idealise them as all knowing and this allows the learner to be dependent and childlike.
- Projective identification is when the parts of the learner projected onto the enabler are attacked to defend against them.
- Transference comes when feelings from a past experience of the learner are being brought into the enabling relationship. Transference usually occurs when the enabler reminds learners of some authority figure from their past such as a parent, teacher or manager. Learners may then react to the enabler as they did to the previous person.
- Counter transference is the name given to feelings that arise in the enabler because of the learner's transferred feelings to them. It is like a self-fulfilling prophecy. The learner sees the enabler in a particular way; the enabler then starts to behave in this way.
- Introjection describes when messages received in childhood are internalised and become part of the way we live. These can be important drivers to an individual's behaviour. The difference in behaviour that would result from the messages given to learners early in their lives such as 'only attempt what you can achieve' or 'have a go, it is the attempt that counts' is self-explanatory.

If problems are occurring in supervision it may well be helpful to involve a third party who can mediate, this could be the university tutor or an experienced practice teacher within the agency.

Learning opportunities not being available

In most social work degree programmes staff invest time in vetting placements to ensure that they provide the required learning opportunities and the enablers are willing and able to undertake their function. Where it can be seen that opportunities may not be readily available, arrangements can be made with other parts of an agency or with other agencies. Sometimes expected work does not materialise and the learner is left not being able to demonstrate competence in a particular area because of a lack of opportunity. This situation may be able to be retrieved by creative thinking on the part of the enabler and it is important to keep an eye on opportunities available so that if a deficit is noted it can be made up elsewhere. If this is not possible it may be that the learner has to have an extension to the number of days in placement and move to another setting for a specific piece of work to allow them to demonstrate. An alternative may be that the learner carries this learning need over to practice at another level if this is feasible and allowed by the educational programme. This would then need to be flagged up as a specific learning need for the next area of practice experience. All these latter alternatives need to be discussed with the social work degree programme and action plans agreed with all parties. On post-qualifying programmes learners use their own workplace to develop their practice. Enablers in these settings may need to negotiate for different opportunities to allow these learners to develop specific skills, for example, practice education.

Personal circumstances of the learner and enabler

Learners in social work and their enablers meet with their fair share of personal difficulty. Illness, either personal or familial, bereavement, accidents, other family tragedies and pregnancy are all common in any group of adults. It is not unknown for enablers to gain promotion, leave an agency or find themselves seconded to another post during a learner's placement. It is therefore advisable for the enabler to consider what alternative arrangements can be made for the learner, should any of these things occur and they are unable to continue in their role. These arrangements should be recorded within the learning agreement. If someone else is to take over from the enabler they will need to be familiar with the progress of the learner and opportunities provided. It would of course be helpful if they were known to the learner and indeed had some involvement with their learning but this is not always possible. They would then need comprehensive notes about the plans the enabler has made for the progression of the learner's learning. Discussion will need to take place between the new enabler and the learner about expectations just as before and this may delay progress on the demonstration of competence. If this is the case a representative from the educational programme should be involved in any arrangements.

When difficulties occur for the learner they may need to be given time out of practice in order to sort these out. Sometimes they have no alternative but to take time away from the practice. Occasionally, they attempt to continue without letting anyone know of their circumstances. Reasons for this may include a lack of trust in their enabler, fear that if they take time out they will fail, a lack of understanding of the impact of their difficulties on their performance or a concern of the financial implications if the time in practice has to be extended. They may manage to continue, but often as they come under stress their work begins to suffer. If they are unwilling to share their difficulties, the enabler has a very difficult job. They should give the learner every opportunity to discuss their difficulties with themselves or suggest they seek help from another source. This could be a tutor from the educational programme or it might be a trusted colleague or in some agencies special care services for staff are available. Evidence in the form of concrete examples should be given to the learner about how their work is being affected if they are unable to accept that the difficulties are having an impact.

Once the enabler knows the extent of the difficulties, negotiations can take place to assist the learner overcome them where possible or for a suspension to the period of practice if this is more appropriate. Learners may have to face difficult decisions such as taking time away from practice, which may mean that they will succeed in the future but have increasing debt and may be out of step with their student cohort. The alternative would be to try to function in less than ideal circumstances, which may lead to failure but would avoid increasing financial burdens. Some learners find themselves in impossible positions and may need specialised help in order to decide on the least-worst alternative. Learners on educational programmes may have access to hardship funds within their educational institutions and knowledge about this could be accessed through tutors. Learners who are employees may well be able to negotiate an appropriate plan of action through team managers involving Human Resources. It is worth taking time to complete these negotiations as they can prevent failure or breakdown, which have far-reaching consequences for all involved. Other less serious factors such as car breakdowns, thefts or computer failure can cause distress for learners who may be on very low incomes and thus not be able to remedy the problem quickly. Enablers should try and put themselves in the learner's position and see if they can help in any way. This might mean allowing them to use agency facilities, negotiating alternative deadlines for pieces of work or renegotiating study time to make it more convenient.

Resistance to learning

Whilst enabling learners in work-based learning, the phenomenon is sometimes noted of learners who raise objections to material offered to them or who do not perform as well as anticipated in certain areas. Atherton (1999) refers to learners who are resistant to some sorts of learning. He argues that resistance takes place when learning is not just 'additive', that is adding generally to the learner's body of knowledge but 'supplantive', that is it replaces existing knowledge or threatens it. Thus when learners are faced with new ideas or ways of working that are at odds with their existing knowledge or ways of working they are threatened. The result of this threat may be avoidance either directly by cancelling sessions, failing to complete work or indirectly by being unable to understand the new ideas – 'being unable to get their head around it' (Atherton, 1999). Greater the emotional investment in the existing knowledge the greater the difficulty the learner may have in trying to change. This can be particularly true of those who have worked for years in unqualified positions within social work and are undertaking a social work education programme or those who are being required unwillingly to undertake post-qualifying training by their agency. Atherton (1999) argues that some of the triggers for resistance to learning are significant, for example, people who are expected to espouse social work values and practices which conflict with deeply held religious views, but that the triggers do not have to be significant. In his research he found that sometimes people in a whole group session found the learning threatening – for example, Race Awareness training which took place in the late 1980s. This often took the form of making participants feel uncomfortable for being born white and for all the ills of the colonial era. In other situations individuals found that different things would trigger resistance. Emotional and cognitive processes seem to work together. Emotions such as anger or despair will inhibit thought processes so that the learner experiences confusion and an inability to grasp concepts that they would normally be able to grasp. Channer (2000) identified Black Christian social work learners who experienced conflict between their religious beliefs and some social work values. She noted that the result of this conflict is a loss or 'traumatic learning' a phrase used initially by Atherton who later changed it to resistance to learning. The learner in this position is in a state of 'crisis' when normal coping mechanisms are not appropriate. The learner may go through three stages, which as in any stage theory merge in and out of each other. Initially they experience destabilisation and then disorientation; they may become depressed and confused. The degree of depression is related to how much a change in beliefs will impact on their lifestyle. We have certainly worked with learners who have found that they are unable to socialise with long-standing friends when they are able to identify that friend's behaviour as racist, sexist, and so on, and are unable to encourage them to change. Sometimes the learner makes the choice to break the relationship; sometimes the other people in the relationship break it off because they cannot stand the constant criticism. Similarly, we have seen long-term intimate relationships in danger of breakdown as the learner challenges established ways of behaving. The learner has to make a decision at this point either to break the relationship or resist the learning totally and leave the programme, or accommodate it by espousing beliefs in their professional lives which do not pass into their private lives. Channer (2000) acknowledges that many Black students find that they have to adopt strategies of personal and political resistance in order to succeed in education. She quotes Gillborn (1990) who regards resistance, accommodation and negotiation as key strategies used by Black students. Professional educators do not always see these strategies as helpful and may challenge the learner's development in these circumstances.

In the final stage in Atherton's model he referred to as 're-orientation', that is the incorporation of the new ideas and so on into the learner's existing modus operandi. This he sees as the end product of success-fully managed traumatic learning. It assumes that only when the new learning is incorporated is the process successful. This goes back to the positivist paradigm of one definition of what is correct and does not acknowledge that the learner could reject the new ideas and return to a state of equilibrium by sticking with their old ideas. Perhaps this would not be acknowledged as learning.

It is important for the enabler to recognise the loss that the learner may undergo when established patterns of working or deeply held beliefs are challenged. In crisis theory it is in the time of destabilisa-tion where the person is most amenable to change. The enablers will need to address their own values in this situation and decide for themselves whether or not assisting change at this time is ethical. Atherton (1999) argues that resistance can also be situational in that learners can object not just to ideas or types of knowledge but to the way it is presented. Learners may not like the teaching methods or the venue or indeed the teacher and may give these as excuses for not getting to grips with the learning. As mentioned in Chapter 3 on Adult Learning it is very important to get these aspects right for learners in order that the learning processes do not inhibit their development.

The enabler may also be resistant to learning as when the learner brings new ideas or ways of working with them, which challenge exist-ing practices. The enabler may well not be able to recognise the learner's competence because they are resistant to the new ways and anxious about change. It might need a third party to intervene where this is the case.

Redeemable mistake, incompetence or malpractice?

Enablers will be faced with learners doing things wrong either by acts of commission or omission. They will need to decide whether this action is a mistake from which the learner should be able to learn or whether it is incompetence or malpractice and the learning should be terminated.

ACTIVITY

Consider the following scenario to help you identify your own views.

Learner A is placed in a voluntary agency undertaking work with a family referred by social services for lack of parenting skills. The plan is for the learner to work with parents on strategies for discipline, boundaries and control of the childrenís behaviour. In the course of discussion of discipline methods, the mother tells the learner that her partner hit one of the children across the mouth when the child was six-months-old. This was several months ago and the mother asks the learner not to mention it to her partner as he gets cross when it is discussed. The learner does not raise the issue with the enabler until their supervision session, which is a week after the discussion with the mother.

Does this incident call into question the learnerís competence and continuation in the placement or is it an area for discussion and a chance to prove that they can work differently in the future?

What would influence your decision?

Consider two more examples given below:

Learner B keeps notes on the families with whom she is working in her diary. On a visit to one family she leaves her diary open and goes out of the room to answer a call on the phone. Later you discover that the family, which the learner was visiting, has taunted a neighbour about their level of debt. The neighbour accuses the learner of breach of confidentiality.

Does this incident call into question the learner's competence and the continuation of the placement or is it an area for discussion and a chance to prove that they can work differently in the future?

What would influence your decision?

Learner C does not turn up in the practice base for a week and does not inform anyone that he will not be in. He returns as though nothing has happened. Does this incident call into question the learner's competence and the continuation of the placement or is it an area for discussion and a chance to prove that he can work differently in the future? What would influence your decision?

In what sort of circumstances would you not give a learner the benefit of another chance but call into being the termination of placement procedures? You might like to discuss these scenarios with colleagues to see if your views are similar or different. It is important for enablers to be familiar with the Codes of Practice for Social Care Workers (GSCC, 2002) so that they are sure of what is generally accepted for workers and therefore learners. Similarly, it is also important to know what matters would result in disciplinary proceedings for workers within an agency. These decisions are complex as not all agencies accept the same standards.

Dealing with learners whose practice is a cause for concern

In the history of social work education failing students have been a relatively rare event (Cowburn et al., 2000). One reason for this may be due to the difficulties this causes the enabler/assessor. Another reason may be the high quality of the process the social work student undertakes. Yet the social work profession has been the subject of numerous inquiries over the years and so it is vitally important that the new registered profession sets high standards for itself and does not admit practitioners who do not meet those standards.

The coming together of the support, development and assessment functions within the enabling role in social work education can lead to difficulties for the enabler and the learner. It is difficult for a learner to perceive someone who is making an assessment on his or her practice as not yet competent. It is often at this point when the learning relationship comes under great strain. We have already highlighted the difficulties which the new enablers face in relation to what is 'good enough' practice for learners in the Chapter 7 on Assessment. Inexperienced enablers may find that they lack confidence in their judgements. This may be exacerbated if the learner raises the issue of the enabler's lack of experience and queries their ability. There is also the possibility that the enabler has unrealistic expectations of what can be achieved in their role. They may take on their own shoulders the total responsibility for the learner's failure. If they think that they are at fault they may not be willing to make a 'fail' decision. It is however clear that in order to qualify as a social worker a learner needs to demonstrate competence in all key roles. If they have not done this, even if there are mitigating circumstances (including the lack of skill on the part of the enabler) they cannot pass. The mitigating circumstances may well lead to an Assessment Board considering that learners should be given another opportunity to demonstrate their competence. Learners have a right to appeal against an Assessment Board decision but an appeal is a statement that the decision made by the Assessment Board is procedurally improper. They cannot usually appeal against a professional judgement. A complaint on the other hand is a statement that learners have not been treated in a way which they were entitled to be. Neither an appeal nor a complaint will overturn a decision of not yet competent, but either could lead to further opportunities being offered to a learner in order for them to demonstrate their competence.

Some enablers may find this system unfair and justify passing a learner because they have not been able to provide the learner with all that they need in order to demonstrate competence. It is a way of assuaging their guilt, real or imagined. It will not however help to gate-keep the standards of the profession. It is possible that the learner, if given another opportunity, will go on to demonstrate competence, but this is unknown at the stage of a 'fail' decision.

Some enablers find difficult to accept the fact that learners have to demonstrate competence in all key roles with no compensation between roles. They may thus accept inadequate demonstration of competence in one area because the learner is good in all other areas. Caution should be taken with this view. Many of the inquiry reports have revealed that unsatisfactory performance in one area such as informing other agencies or recording information have led to serious problems for service users. The key roles are just that, areas in which all qualified social workers should be competent in order to do their job. One role is not more important than another; they all have equal weight.

The implications of failure for a learner may impact on an enabler's decision. Extra time and finances are required to undertake further learning opportunities. In the case of a learner on a Post-qualifying programme or an employment route to qualification this may or may not be negotiated with the employer. If it is not it might lead to resent-ment by the employee and inappropriate judgements being made by colleagues who do not understand the full story and only hear that the learner has failed. The enabler may be blamed for the learners not achieving competence and not receiving remuneration or status which they think they were due. This can lead to tensions in a team or agency if the failed learner and the enabler remain working together. Learners who are on degree programmes may have to wait for a further learning opportunity. This puts a strain on finances and may mean that a learner cannot progress with his or her cohort. Several students we have worked with have calculated how much money they have lost by not being able to qualify (sometimes through no fault of their own). At least one threatened to sue for lost earnings. This pressure can be difficult for enablers to bear particularly when they can see that the blame for the learner's failure does not just lie with the learner.

Tutors from educational programmes have been known to make their own judgements about students based on their experience of them in the classroom and from their academic work. Their incredulity that an enabler may be failing a learner who they consider to be good can knock the confidence of the enabler particularly when other issues of power differentials are present All these factors can lead to emotional pressure on an enabler not to make a 'fail' decision. It requires some strength of character and a lot of support to continue with a 'fail' decision in the face of such pressure. Both the enabler and the learner need ongoing support systems in these circumstances. 'Failing a student on practice grounds can get very messy and emotionally fraught, carrying the threat of appeal or even litigation from the student' (Sharp and Danbury, 1999, p. 147).

ACTIVITY

To prepare for the feelings which may be engendered when a learner is told that they are not making the required progress.

Think several times about when you have had to point out to someone that their behaviour is not acceptable.

How did you feel?
What factors made it harder for you in some of the situations?
What factors made it easier for you in some of the situations?
Would anything have prevented you from raising the issue at all?

Think about times when you have been told that you could do better or that you have failed to do something correctly.

How did you feel?
How did you respond?
What factors affected your response?

Some of the feelings which surface are very strong and include shock, disbelief, anger, depression, blame, guilt and avoidance. Being prepared for the feelings means that they are less likely to takeover.

Naming concerns

Enablers should bring their concerns to the attention of the learner as soon as possible. Enablers will need time to formulate their thoughts and to clarify their concerns. These could be concerns about the learner's competence in relation to one or more of the key roles, concerns about the learner's value base or concern about the learner's level of knowledge. Once they have established the area in which the concern lies they should name the issues giving specific examples. It is no good saying to a learner that their communication skills are poor. They will need to know which communication skills and in what circumstances and why the enabler considered them to be poor. Examples of what is expected in that situation would be helpful for comparison. The message should be given straightforwardly, not dressed up with lots of excuses and not be lost at this point by acknowledging the learner's feelings. This can be done later when the message has been received (Danbury and Sharp 1999). The enabler should check that the learner has understood the enabler's concern and give the learner the opportunity to say how they perceive the situation. Discussion should take place with the learner to see if there is a way through the issue. For example, can remedial action be taken? Following this an action plan should be devised with the learner. If appropriate and necessary a representative of the educational programme should be included in the plan. The plan should set timescales and review progress. The enabler should be clear with the learner about possible consequences if concerns remain after the action plan is implemented. The whole process should be recorded clearly and a check made that the learner agrees with the record.

Learners will respond to concerns in different ways. Some will go on to demonstrate competence, others will improve but not sufficiently to demonstrate competence, others will not improve at all. The enabler will have to decide towards the end of the learner's time in practice whether or not any progress made is sufficient for them to recommend that the learner is competent. If they deem the learner to be competent they will write a report according to educational programme specifications. If they consider that the learner is not yet competent the report will need to identify clearly the areas of difficulty, the strategies that have been put in place to assist the learner, and the areas in which the learner has achieved competence. The report will be considered by the Assessment Board of any educational programme in order to decide whether or not the learner should be given an extension to the learning opportunity or another opportunity to demonstrate his or her competence. Their decision will be based on whether or not there have been difficulties in the learning opportunities offered, the learning relationship or any other mitigating circumstances. If these difficulties have hindered learner progress they may well be given another learning opportunity. If this is the case it is usual practice for the enabler in the new practice setting to be given the report from the previous setting. It is therefore important to be clear about the areas of difficulty so that all parties can understand the learner's particular learning needs for this new opportunity. Learners sometimes find this process difficult. They argue that the report will prejudice the new enabler against them. It is therefore important that the new enabler discusses the report with the learner and reassures them that they will be starting with a clean slate.

Key Learning Points

- Prevention is better than cure and careful preparation, thought and clear recording can help prevent problems.
- Early identification of difficulties can help problems becoming more severe or entrenched.
- Many difficulties can be overcome with honesty, openness and a willingness to be creative and supportive.
- Where difficulties persist the situation can become fraught and support is needed for both learner and enabler.
- Understanding the procedures set in place by educational programmes can help facilitate the process to either resolve difficulties or make a decision for not yet competent or failure.
- Learners should not be allowed to pass unless they have demonstrated competence in all areas whatever the mitigating circumstances. We have professional credibility and the service to users to consider.

Conclusion

Through the chapters of this book we have introduced the reader to the key components of successful programmes of learning in the social care workplace. The concept of 'learning to learn' has been central to the book, and we hope that it will help the busy people of Schön's 'swampy lowland', learners and enablers alike, to develop the skills which will set them up as lifelong learners. Continual professional development is no longer a luxury to be indulged by the privileged few, but a necessity for all workers within the sector. As social care strives to respond to the changing needs of the population, the changing requirements of legislation, policy and procedure, and the changing environment of multi-professional working, the workforce in it needs to be adaptable, well trained and continually developing. Furthermore, the workforce needs to equip itself to be a driver for those changes that particularly affect service delivery, and moving beyond the merely re-active to being constructively proactive in shaping the services it delivers. Only in this way can we truly say that we are working in the service user's best interests. *Enablers should be (and should develop) agitators.*

Social care organisations need to be full of enablers of learning, embracing those willing to learn. Employers need to fully recognise this fact and facilitate the variety of enablers needed within an organisation. There will be different roles for enablers at different levels of expertise. It is essential for the profession that these different roles are identified and linked to suitable qualifications (Higham, 2006). The roles may be packaged differently and given different names within organisations but essentially they will all contain some of the elements discussed in this book. It is no longer sufficient to place learners next to an experienced worker and expect the worker to pass on all his or her knowledge and skills to the learners. Organisations are rapidly changing and we need adaptable workers, not clones of existing workers. Assessment against occupational standards and the emphasis on competence is in danger of producing workers who 'paint by numbers' rather than create and innovate: 'sound professional practice is not based on narrow competence in carrying out today's tasks, but in a rational ability to apply existing knowledge and thinking in seeking solutions to new problems' (Thompson, 2002, p. 153).

Enablers need to encourage learners to be reflective and creative when undertaking work with users of service and in contributing to the functioning of the organisation within which they work. Enablers should also encourage learners to transfer skills from other areas of expertise and build on them for the future – just as they should themselves. The literature around practice learning for social work places a huge importance on the enabler as pivotal to the success of learning in practice (Dick, Headrick and Scott, 2002). Enablers need to seize this role and shape it in a way that promotes the values of the profession and creates the types of workers who will *make a difference.*

Members of the social care workforce are increasingly likely to find themselves working in multidisciplinary settings. We see the enabler as the fulcrum for inter-professional learning and practice. They are well placed to encourage the sharing of knowledge and skills between members of different professions. *Enablers should be (and should develop) negotiators.* They can transfer their skills of liaison with others when setting up learning opportunities across the professional divides looking for commonalties and difference. Working alongside other professionals in one setting does not necessarily mean working together to best effect for service users. The enabler in these settings can encourage the learner to develop their own professional identify whilst understanding that other professions have their own values, identities and modus operandi. Enablers in these settings are also best placed to encourage learners to develop research skills. This may lead to projects which enhance service provision or may just involve effective evaluation of practice. In these ways learners can be encouraged to give something of value to the service in which they are placed to learn, and thus to the people who are using that service. *Enablers should be (and should develop) researchers.*

Many enablers we work with find the role enhances their own practice and gives them added expertise and job satisfaction. We believe that being prepared for the role will reduce difficulties and enhance the experience of both learner and enabler alike. This book was developed to prepare enablers for their task and give them ideas to facilitate the learners' progress and extend their own expertise as enablers. We have stressed throughout that preparation and planning is key to successful work-based learning, but they will not ensure success by themselves. Difficulties which have not been anticipated will always occur. The enabler will learn from working through these difficulties, but they will need support. This support should not be left to chance. If we take the matter of continual professional development seriously then this should cover all aspects of our development including work as an enabler. We have much to learn from each other and from reflecting on our own and other's practice. We hope we have aroused your interest in workplace learning and that you will have a stimulating and interesting experience of enabling, and promoting the values of our profession.

Glossary

Codes of Practice

These are published by all the Social Care Councils which govern the four countries of the United Kingdom. They contain requirements for both Social Care Employers and Social Care employees. Failure to comply with the Code as a social care employee could lead to deregistration

Continual Professional Development (CPD)

Most professions have required their members to continually improve their knowledge and skills. Social Workers are now required to demonstrate that they are doing this on a regular basis as a requirement for re-registration on the Social Care Council's register.

Enabler

A generic term used in the text to describe the person who has responsibility for assisting another to develop their professional practice. They may have specific titles such as mentor, practice teacher, practice assessor, and supervisor. These people may have slightly differing emphasis in their role (support, teaching, assessment and so forth), but they all have in common the function of enabling a learner to develop knowledge, skills and values.

Learner

The term used to describe the persons who are working with the enabler to develop their knowledge, skills and values. They may be formally registered on an education programme such as a social work degree or post-qualifying award, but not necessarily so. They may be undertaking some work within their agency to develop their skills and knowledge in a new area. The term is used in preference to the word student so that it does not exclude the people who are still learning but in a more informal way.

Learning Opportunity

The chances provided to learners to help them develop knowledge, skills and values. They may have several chances in one setting or the chances may be scattered across different settings.

Mentee

The learner working with a mentor

Mentor

Traditionally this term has described the person who has passed on their knowledge and skills to their mentee. Whilst the term can have many meanings, we use it to describe the enabler who generally does not have an assessment function within their role. The relationship between learner and enabler in mentoring is more of an alliance than a hierarchy; the emphasis is more on learning than assessing against standards.

National Occupational Standards (NOS)

The requirements which people must meet in order to satisfy the professional body that they are competent and eligible for registration.

Placement

A series of learning opportunities offered in one particular setting.

Post-Qualifying (PQ)

Learning which is undertaken after the basic qualifying education and training has been completed.

Practice Assessor

A term which is often used synonymously with practice teaching but perhaps emphasises the assessment function within the role over the teaching and learning function. In some professions the two functions are separated out and given to different people, but in social work these functions generally reside within the one role.

Practice Teacher

The person who teaches, assesses and supports a student on a social work degree programme whilst they are on placement. More then one person may be involved in providing this role

Private Voluntary and Independent Sector (PVI)

Agencies which provide social work and/or social care services to the public but are not directly financed and regulated by central government through statute and guidance.

Social Work Education Programme

Formal programmes of study provided generally by Higher Education Institutions which lead to specific qualifications in social work either at qualifying or post-qualifying levels.

Statutory Sector

Agencies providing social work/social care services directly financed and regulated by central government through stature and guidance

Student

A learner registered on a social work education programme

Tutor

Person designated by a social work education programme to assist a student with their learning within the university and support them whilst on placement. There may be more than one tutor assigned to a student as sometimes different people offer support during placement to those assisting learning whilst in university.

Bibliography

Adams, R., Dominelli, L. and Payne, M. (eds) (2002) *Critical Practice in Social Work*. Basingstoke: Palgrave.

Allinson, C. and Hayes, J. (1996) The Cognitive Styles Index, *Journal of Management Studies*, 33, pp. 119–135.

Apter, M. (2001) *Motivational Styles in Everyday life: A Guide to Reversal Theory*. Washington DC: American Psychological Association.

Argyris, C. and Schön, D. (1978) *Organizational Learning: A Theory of Action Perspective*. Reading, Mass: Addison Wesley.

Atherton, J. (1999) Resistance to Learning: A Discussion Based on Participants in In-Service Professional Training Programmes, *Journal of Vocational Education and Training*, 5 (1), pp. 17–93.

Baldwin, M. and Burgess, H. (1992) Enquiry and Action Learning in Practice Placements, *Social Work Education*, 11 (3), pp. 36–44.

Barnes, S. and Bulman, C. (2001) *Reflective Practice in Nursing*. Oxford: Blackwell.

Barron, C. (2004) Fair Play: Creating a Better Learning Climate for Social Work Students in Social Care Settings, *Social Work Education*, 23 (1), pp. 25–37.

Bartram, S. and Gibson, B. (1993) *Developing Training Skills*. Aldershot: Connaught Training.

Beale, S. (2005) *Preparation for Placement Workbook*. Manchester: Manchester Metropolitan University.

Belardi, N. (2002) Social Work Supervision in Germany, *European Journal of Social Work*, 5 (3), pp. 313–318.

Bloom, B.S. (1956) *Taxonomy of Educational Objectives*. London: Longman.

Boud, D., Keogh, R. and Walker, D. (1985) *Reflection: Turning Experience into Learning*. London: Kogan Paul.

Bradley, H. (2002) *Fractured Identities: Changing Patters of Inequality, Gender and Power in the Workplace*. Cambridge: Polity Press.

Brockbank, A. and McGill, I. (1998) *Facilitating Reflective Learning in Higher Education*. Buckingham: Open University Press.

Brookfield, S. (1986) *Understanding and Facilitating Adult Learning*. San Francisco: Jossey Bass.

Brown, S. and Knight, P. (1994) *Assessing Learners in Higher Education*. London: Kogan Page.

Burns, S. and Bullman, C. (eds) (2000) *Reflective Practice in Nursing (The Growth of the Professional Practitioner)* 2nd edn. Oxford: Blackwell Science.

Cartney, P. (2000) Adult Learning Styles: Implications for Practice Teaching in Social Work, *Social Work Education*, 19 (6), pp. 609–627.

Castells, M. (2001) Information Technology and Global Capitalism. In Hutton W. and Giddens, A. (eds) *On the Edge. Living with Global Capitalism*. London: Vintage.

CCETSW (1996) *Guidance on the 'Long-arm' Model of Practice Teaching* (revised) London : CCETSW.

Channer, Y. (2000) Understanding and Managing Conflict in the Learning Process: Christians Coming Out. In Cree, V. and Macaulay, C. (2000) *Transfer of Learning in Professional and Vocational Education*. London: Routledge.

Cheetham, J. and Kazi A.F. Mansoor (1998) *The Working of Social Work*. London: Jessica Kingsley.

Children Act 1989 (c.41). London: HMSO

Children Act 2004 (c.31). London: HMSO

Clark, C.L. (2000) *Social Work Ethics, Politics, Principles and Practice*. Basingstoke: Macmillan.

Clegg, S. (1999) Professional Education, Reflective Practice and Feminism, *International Journal of Inclusive Education* 1999, 3 (2), pp. 167–179.

Clutterbuck, D. (2004) *Everyone Needs a Mentor: Fostering Talent in Your Organisation*. Wiltshire: Chartered Institute of Personnel Development, Cromwell Press.

Coffield, F., Moseley, D., Hall, E. and Ecclestone, K. (2004) *Should We Be Using Learning Styles? What Research has to Say to Practice?* London: Learning and Skills Research Centre.

Cousins, C. (2004) Becoming a Social Work Supervisor: A Significant Role in Transition, *Australian Social Work*, June 2004, 57 (2), pp. 175–195.

Cowburn, M., Nelson, P. and Williams, J. (2000) Assessment of Social Work Students Standpoint and Strong Objectivity, *Social Work Education*, 19 (6), pp. 627–639.

Cowen, H. (1999) *Community Care, Ideology and Social Policy*. London: Prentice Hall.

Cree, V. and Macauley, C. (eds) (2000) *Transfer of Learning in Professional and Vocational Education*. London: Routledge.

Crisp, B.R. and Lister, P.G. (2003) Literature Review on Assessment Methods, *Social Work Education Social*, 23 (2), pp. 199–217.

Danbury, H. and Sharp, M. (1999) *The Management of Failing DipSW Students*. Aldershot: Ashgate.

Dempsey, M., Halton, C. and Murphy, M. (2001) Reflective Learning in Social Work Education: Scaffolding the Process, *Social Work Education*, 20 (6), pp. 631–641.

Department of Health (1998) *Partnership in Action*. London: HMSO.

Department of Health (2002) *Requirements for Social Work Training*. London: HMSO.

Department of Health (2003) *Every Child Matters*. London: HMSO.

Department of Health (2005) *Personal Social Services Staff of Social Services Department at 30th September 2004 England*. Department of Health (http://www.dh.gov.uk/PublicationsAndStatistics) accessed August 2005.

Department of Health (2005) *Independence Well Being and Choice*. London: HMSO.

Department of Health and the English National Board (2001) *Placements in Focus: Guidance for Education in Practice for Health Care Professions*. London: HMSO.

Department of Health/DfES (2006) *Options for Excellence – Building the Social Care Workforce of the Future*. London: COI

Devine, F. and Heath, S. (1999) *Sociological Research Methods in Context*. Basingstoke: Palgrave.

Dewey, J. (1933) *How We Think*. Boston: Heath & Co.

Dick, E., Hendrick, D. and Scott, M. (2002) *Practice Learning for Professional Skills: A review of the literature*. Edinburgh: Scottish Executive.

Disability Discrimination Act 1995 (c.50). London: HMSO.

Doel, M. (2000) Practice Teaching and Learning. In Pierce, R. and Weinstein, J. (2000) *Innovative Education and Training for Care Professionals: A Providers Guide*. London: Jessica Kingsley.

Doel, M. (2005) *New Approaches to Practice Learning*. London: Practice Learning Taskforce.

Doel, M. and Shardlow, S. (1998) *The New Social Work Practice: Exercises and Activities for Training and Developing Social Workers*. Arena: Aldershot.

Doel, M., Sawdon, C. and Morrison, D. (2002) *Learning, Practice and Assessment: Signposting the portfolio*. London: Jessica Kingsley.

Dominelli, L. (1996) Deprofessionalising social work: anti-oppressive practice, competencies and postmodernism, *British Journal of Social Work*, 26 (2), pp. 153–175.

Dominelli, L. (2004) *Social Work*. Cambridge: Polity Press.

Donley, J. and Napper, R. (1999) *Assessment Matters in Adult Learning*. Oxford: Oxfordshire Country Council and National Institute of Adult and Continuing Education.

Drakeford, M. (2006) *Governmental Review of Social Work*. Presentation to Third Assembly Forum 22nd May. Birmingham: BASW.

Dunn, R. (2003) The Dunn and Dunn Learning Style Model and its Theoretical Cornerstone. In Dunn, R. and Griggs, S. (eds) *Synthesis of the Dunn and Dunn Learning Styles Model and Research*. New York: St Johns University.

Dunn, R. and Griggs, S. (2003) *Synthesis of the Dunn and Dunn Learning Styles Model and Research*. New York: St Johns University.

Durkin, C. and Shergill, M. (2000) A Team Approach to Practice Teaching, *Social Work Education*, 19 (2), pp. 165–174.

Earwaker, J. (1992) *Helping and Supporting Students: Rethinking the Issues*. Buckingham: The Society for Research into Higher Education and Open University Press.

Edwards, C. (2003) The Involvement of Service Users in the Assessment of Diploma in Social Work Students on Practice Placements, *Social Work Education*, 22 (4), pp. 341–349.

Entwhistle, N. (1996) Recent Research on Student Learning and the Learning Environment. In Tait, J. and Knight, P. (eds) *The Management of Independent Learning*. London: Kogan Page.

Entwhistle, N., McClune, V. and Walker, P. (2001) Conceptions, Styles and Approaches Within Higher Education; Analytical Abstraction and Everyday Experience. In Sternberg, R.J. and Zhang, L.F. (eds) *Perspectives on Thinking, Learning and Cognitive Styles*. London: Lawrence Eribaum.

Eraut, M. (1994) *Developing Professional Knowledge and Competence*. London: Falmer Press.

Etzioni, A. (ed.) (1969) *The Semi-Professions and Their Organisation: Teachers, Nurses, Social Workers*. New York: Free Press.

Evans, D. (1999) *Practice Learning in the Caring Professions*. Aldershot: Ashgate Arena.

Evans, T. and Harris, J. (2004) Street Level Bureaucracy, Social Work and the Exaggerated Death of Discretion, *British Journal of Social Work*, 34 (6), pp. 871–895.

Fernandez, E. (1998) Students Perceptions of Satisfaction with Practicum Learning, *Social Work Education*, 17 (2), pp. 173–203.

Fisher, T. and Somerton, J. (2000) Reflection on Action: The Process of Helping Social Work Students to Develop Their Use of Theory in Practice, *Social Work Education*, 19 (4), pp. 387–401.

Fook, J. (1996) *The Reflective Researcher*. New South Wales: Allen and Unwin St Leonrads.

Fook, J. (2002) *Social Work: Critical Theory and Practice*. London: Sage.

Ford, K. and Jones, A. (1987) *Student Supervision*. Basingstoke: BASW MacMillan.

Freire, P. (1972) *Pedagogy of the Oppressed*. London: Penguin.

Freire, P. (1973) *Education: The Practice of Freedom*. London: Writers and Readers Publishing Co-operative.

Freire, P. (1985) *The Politics of Education: Culture, Power and Liberation*. London: Macmillan.

French, J.P.R. Jr. and Raven, B. (1960) The Bases of Social Power. In Cartwright, D. and Zander, A. (eds) *Group dynamics*, pp. 607–623. New York: Harper and Row.

Friedson, E. (1994) *Professionalism Reborn: Theory, Prophecy and Policy*. Cambridge: Polity Press.

Frost, N., Robinson, M. and Anning, A. (2005) Social Workers in Multidiscplinary teams: Issues and Dilemmas for Professional Practice, *Child and Family Social Work*, 10, pp. 187–196.

Gardiner, D. (1989) *The Anatomy of Supervision: Developing Learning and Professional Competence for Social Work Students*. Bury St Edmonds: The Society for Research Into Higher Education Open University Press.

General Social Care Council (2002) *Accreditation of Universities to Grant Degrees in Social Work*. London: GSCC.

General Social Care Council (2002) *Code of Practice*. London: GSCC.

General Social Care Council (2003) *Statement of Commitment*. London: GSCC.

General Social Care Council (2005) *Specialist Standards and Requirements for Post Qualifying Social Work Education and Training: Children and Young People, their Families and Carers*. London: GSCC.

General Social Care Council (2005) *Revised Post Qualifying Framework for Social Work*. London: GSCC.

General Social Care Council and Training Organisation for the Personal Social Services (2002) *Guidance on the Assessment of Practice in the Workplace.* London: GSCC.

Gibbs, G. (1995) *Learning by Doing.* London: FEU Publications.

Gibb, S. (2002) *Leaning and Development: Processes, Practices and Perspectives at Work.* Basingstoke: Palgrave Macmillan.

Gillborn, D. (1990) *Race, Ethnicity and Education.* London: Unwin Hayman.

Glasby, J. (2003) Bringing Down the Berlin Wall: the Health and Social Care Divide, *British Journal of Social Work*, 33 (7), pp. 969–975.

Gould, N. and Taylor, I. (eds) (1996) *Reflective Learning for Social Work Research, Theory and Practice.* England: Arena.

Gray, D. (2001) A *Briefing on Work-based Learning.* Assessment Series 11. Learning Teaching Support Network Generic Centre (accessed through www.bioscience.heacademy.ac.uk).

Greenwood, E. (1957) Attributes of a Profession, *Social Work*, 2 (3), pp. 8–19.

Gregory, M. and Holloway, M. (2005) Language and the Shaping of Social Work, *British Journal of Social Work*, 35, pp. 37–53.

Gutierrez, L.M. (1990) Working with Women of Color: An Empowerment Perspective, *Social Work*, 35 (2), pp. 149–153.

Hammond, M. and Collins, R. (1997) *Self Directed Learning.* London: Kogan Page.

Harvey, L. (1990) *Critical Social Research.* London: Unwin Hyman.

Hawkins, P. and Shohet, R. (2000) *Supervision in the Helping Professions.* Buckingham: Open University Press.

Henkel, M. (1995) Conceptions of Knowledge and Social Work Education. In Yelloly, M. & Henkel, M. (eds) *Learning and Teaching in Social Work.* London: Jessica Kingsley Publishers.

Hermann, N. (1989) *The Creative Brain.* North Carolina: Brain Books, The Ned Hermann Group.

Heron, J. (1989) *The Facilitator's Handbook.* London: Kogan Page.

Higham, P. (2006) *The Challenge of Modernisation: How Social Work is Developing a New Professionalism for Social Work.* Keynote address National Organisation for Practice Teaching conference 12th Sept. Manchester.

Hinchliff, S. (ed.) (1999) *The Practitioner as Teacher.* London: Balliere Tindall.

HMSO (2002) *Working Together: Effective Partnership Working on the Ground.* England: Public Services Productivity Panel HM Treasury.

Home Office (2002) *Improving Partnerships.* England: HMSO.

Honey, P. and Mumford, A. (1996) *Building a Learning Environment.* Maidenhead: Peter Honey Publications Ltd.

Howe, D. (1994) Modernity, Post modernity and Social Work, *British Journal of Social Work*, 24 (5), pp. 513–532.

Hudson, B., Hardy, B., Henwood, M. and Wistow G. (1997) *Interagency Collaboration: Final Report.* Leeds: Nuffield Institute for Health.

Hughes, E.C. (1984) *The Sociological Eye.* New Brunswick, NJ: Transaction Publishers.

Hugman, R. (2005) Looking Back: The View from Here, *British Journal of Social Work*, 35, pp. 609–620.

Hunt, C. (2001) Shifting Shadows: Metaphors and Maps for Facilitating Reflective Practice, *Reflective Practice*, 2 (3), pp. 275–287.

Ixer, G. (1999) There's No Such Thing as Reflection, *British Journal of Social Work*, 29, pp. 513–527.

Jarvis, P. (1987) *Adult Learning in the Social Context*. London : Croom Helm.

Jarvis, P. (1996) *The Adult Learner and Adult Learning*. London: Routledge.

Jarvis, P. and Gibson, S. (1997) *The Teacher Practitioner and Mentor in Nursing, Midwifery, Health Visiting and the Social Services*. Cheltenham: Stanley Thornes.

Jordan, B. (2001) Tough Love: Social Work, Social Exclusion and the Third Way, *British Journal of Social Work*, 31, pp. 527–546.

Kadushin, A. (1976) *Supervision in Social Work*. New York: Columbia University Press.

Kemshall, H. and Pritchard, J. (eds) (1996) *Good Practice in Risk Assessment and Risk Management*. London: Jessica Kingsley.

Kerka, S. (1995) *The Learning Organization: Myths and Realities*. Columbus, OH: Eric Clearing House.

Knowles, M.S. (1980) *The Modern Practice of Adult Education: Andragogy Versus Pedagogy*. Englewood Cliffs: Prentice Hall/ Cambridge.

Kolb, D.A. (1975) Towards an Applied Theory of Experiential Learning. In Cooper, C. (ed.) *Theories of Group Processes*. London: Wiley.

Kolb, D.A. (1983) *Experiential Learning: Experience on the Source of Learning and Development*. New York: Prentice Hall.

Kolb, D.A. (1999) *The Kolb Learning Styles Inventory version 3*. Boston: Hay Group.

Kondrat, M.E. (1999) Who is the Self in Self Awareness from Critical Theory Perspective? *Social Services Review*, 73, pp. 451–477.

Lawson, H. (ed.) (1998) *Practice Teaching-Changing Social Work*. London: Jessica Kingsley.

Lee, D. (1998) Sexual Harassment in PhD Supervision, *Gender and Education*, 10 (3), pp. 299–312.

Lindsey, T. (2005) Group Learning on Social Work Placements, *Groupwork*, 15 (1), pp. 61–89.

Littler, L. (2005) *Practice Teaching Training Workshop*. Unpublished manuscript, Manchester University

Longenecker, L. (2002) The Jotter Wallet: Invoking Reflective Practice in a Family Practice Residency Program (with a commentary by Levine, C.), *Reflective Practice*, 3 (2), pp. 219–224.

Low, H. and Weinstein, J. (2000) Interprofessional Education. In Pierce, R. and Weinstein, J. (eds) *Innovative Education and Training for Care Professionals: A Providers Guide*. London: Jessica Kingsley.

Lucas, B. (2002) *Power Up Your Mind: Learn Faster Work Smarter*. London: Nicholas Brearley.

Lymbery, M. and Butler, S. (2004) *Social Work Ideals and Practice Realit*, Basingstoke: Palgrave Macmillan.

Macleod-Clark, J., Maben, J. and Jones, K. (1996) *Project 2000, Perceptions of the Philosophy and Practice of Nursing*. London: English National Board for Nursing Midwifery and Health Visiting.

Maidment, J. and Cooper, L. (2002) Acknowledgment of Client Diversity and Oppression in Social Work Student Supervision, *Social Work Education*, 21 (4), pp. 399–407.

Mantell, A. (1998) 'On Shifting Sands: Student Social Workers' Experiences of Working in Multi-Disciplinary Teams, Chapter 11. In Lawson, H. (ed.) *Practice Teaching: Changing Social Work*. London: Jessica Kingsley.

Marsick, V.J. and Watkins, K. (1990) *Informal and Incidental Learning in the Workplace*. London: Routledge.

Maslow, A. (1986) *Towards a Psychology of Being*. New York: Van Nostrand.

Mattick, K. and Bligh, J. (2006) Getting the Measure of Interprofessional Learning, *Medical Education*, 40, pp. 399–400.

McCrystal, P. and Godfrey, A. (2001) Developing a Researcher-Practitioner Partnership for the Effective Evaluation of Professional Social Work Training, *Social Work Education*, 20 (5), pp. 539–550.

McHale, E. and Carr, A. (1998) The Effect of Supervisor and Trainee Therapist Gender on Supervision Discourse, *Journal of Family Therapy*, 20, pp. 395–411.

McIvor, G. (ed.) (1996) *Working with Offenders: Research Highlights in Social Work*. London: Jessica Kingsley.

McLeod, J. (1999) *Practitioner Research in Counselling*. Sage: London.

Melton, R. (1997) *Objectives, Competences and Learning Outcomes Developing Instructional Materials in Open and Distance Learning*. London: Kogan Page.

Merton, R.R., Reader, G.G. and Kendall, P.L. (eds) (1957) *The Student Physician: Introductory Studies in the Sociology of Medical Education*. Cambridge MA: Harvard University Press.

Mezirow, J. (1981) A Critical Theory of Adult Learning and Education, *Adult Education*, 32 (1), pp. 3–24.

Mezirow, J. and Associates (1990) *Fostering Critical Reflection in Adulthood: A Guide to Transformative and Emancipatory Learning*. San Francisco: Jossey-Bass.

Miller, A.H., Imrie, B.W. and Cox, K. (1998) *Student Assessment in Higher Education*. London: Kogan Page.

Moon, J.A. (1999) *Learning Journals: A Handbook for Academics, Students and Professional Development*. London: Kogan Page.

Morrison, T. (2002) *Staff Supervision in Social Care: Making a Real Difference for Staff and Service Users*. Brighton: Pavillion.

Myers, I.B. and Mc Caulley, M.H. (1985) *Manual: A Guide to the Development and Use of the Myers-Briggs Type Indicator*. Palo Alto, CA: Consulting Psychologists Press.

National Health Service and Community Care Act 1990 (c.19). London: HMSO

O'Hagan, K. (1996) *Competence in Social Work Practice: A Practical Guide for Professionals*. Bristol: Jessica Kingsley.

Olesen, V.L. and Whittaker E.W. (1970) Critical Notes on Sociological Studies on Professional Socialisation. In Jackson, J. (ed.) *Professions and Professionalisation*. London: Cambridge University Press.

Palmer, A.M., Burns, S. and Bulman, C. (1994) *Reflective Practice in Nursing: The Growth of the Professional Practitioner*. Oxford: Blackwell Science Publications.

Parker, J. (2004) *Effective Practice Learning in Social Work*. Exeter: Learning Matters.

Parsloe, P. (2001) Looking back on social work education, *Social Work Education*, 20 (1), pp. 9–19.

Parton, N. (1994) Problematics of Government: (post) Modernity and Social Work, *British Journal of Social Work*, 24 (1), pp. 9–32.

Payne, M. (1991) *Modern Social Work Theory: A Critical Introduction*. Basingstoke: Macmillan.

Payne, M. (1998) Social Work Theories and Reflective Practice. In Adams, R., Dominelli, L. and Payne, M. (eds) *Social Work: Themes, Issues and Critical Debates*. London: Macmillan.

Pegg, M. (1999) *The Art of Mentoring*. Chalford: Management Books 2000.

Petty, G. (2005) *Teaching Today* (3rd Edition). Cheltenham: Stanley Thornes.

Phillipson, J. (2002) Supervision and Being Supervised, Chapter 24. In Adams, R., Dominelli, L. and Payne, M. (eds) (2002) *Critical Practice in Social Work*. Basingstoke: Palgrave.

Pierce, R. and Weinstein, J. (2000) *Innovative Education and Training for Care Professionals: A Providers Guide*. London: Jessica Kingsley.

Pinker, R. (1997) Recent Trends in British Social Policy and their Implications for Social Work Practice and Education, *Issues in Social Work Education*, 17 (2), pp. 15–36.

Pollard, K., Miers, M. and Gilchrist, M. (2004) Collaborative Learning for Collaborative Working? Initial Findings from a Longitudinal Study of Health and Social Care Education, *Health and Social Care in the Community*, 12 (4), pp. 346–358.

Prestonshoot, M. and Williams, J. (1995) Evaluating the Effectiveness of Practice, *Social Work Practice*, 1 (4), pp. 393–405.

Race, P. (2002) *The Lecturers Toolkit*. London: Kogan Page.

Raelin, J. (2000) *Workbased Learning: The New Frontier of Management Development*. New Jersey: Prentice Hall.

Raelin, J. (2002). 'I Don't Have Time to Think!' Versus the Art of Reflective Practice, *Reflections*, 4 (1), pp. 66–79. Cambridge, MA: Society for Organizational Learning, Massachusetts Institute of Technology.

Redmond, B. (2004) *Reflection in Action: Developing Reflective Practice in Health and Social Services*. Aldershot: Ashgate.

Reece, I. and Walker, S. (2000) *Teaching, Training and Learning: A Practical Guide*. Sunderland: Tyne and Wear Business Educational Publishers Ltd.

Ringel, S. (2001) In the Shadow of Death: Relational Paradigms in Clinical Supervision, *Clinical Social Work Journal*, 29 (2), pp. 171–179.

Rogers, C. (1969) *Freedom to Learn: A View of What Education Might Become.* Ohio: CE Merrill.

Rosenstein, B. (2002) The Sorcerer's Apprentice and the Reflective Practitioner, *Reflective Practice*, 3 (3), pp. 255–261.

Rowlings, C. (2000) Social Work Education and Higher Education: Mind the Gap. In Pierce, R. and Weinstein, J. *Innovative Education and Training for Care Professionals: A Providers Guide.* Chapter 3, pp. 61–80. London: Jessica Kingsley.

Rowntree, D. (1987) *Assessing Students: How Shall We Know Them?* London: Kogan Page.

Ruch, G. (2002) From Triangle to Spiral: Reflective Practice in Social Work Education, Practice and Research, *Social Work Education*, 21 (2), pp. 199–216.

Rynanen, K. (2001) *Constructing Physicians Professional Identity – exploration of students critical experience in medical education.* Helsinki: Oulu University Press.

Salaman, G. (1995) *Managing: Managing Work and Organisations.* Buckingham: Open University Press.

Schön, D. (1983) *The Reflective Practitioner: How Professionals Think in Action.* London: Temple Smith.

Schön, D.A. (1973) *Beyond the Stable State: Public and Private Learning in a Changing Society.* Harmondsworth: Penguin.

Schulman, L. (1982) *Skills of Supervision and Staff.* Chicago IL: Management Peacock Publications.

Schulman, L. (1984) *The Skills of Helping: Individuals and Groups* (2nd edition). Itasca, IL: Peacock.

SCIE (2004) *Resource Guide 2 Involving Service Users in Social Work Education.* London: SCIE.

Scottish Executive (2006) *Changing Lives. Report of the 21st Century Review of Social Work.* Edinburgh: Scottish Executive.

Seidel, S. and Blythe, T. (1996) *Reflective Practice in the Classroom.* Unpublished article, Project Zero/ Massachusetts Schools Network.

Senge, P.M. (1990) *The Fifth Discipline: The Art and Practice of the Learning Organization.* London: Random House.

Shardlow, S. and Doel, M. (1996) *Practice Learning and Teaching.* London: Macmillan.

Sharp, M. and Danbury, H. (1999) *The Management of Failing DipSW Students: Activities and Exercises to Prepare Practice Teachers For Work With Failing Students.* London: Ashgate.

Shaw, I. (1997) *Be Your Own Evaluator: A Guide to Reflective and Enabling Intervention.* Wrexham: Prospects Training Publications.

Shaw, I. (1999) *Qualitative Evaluation (Introducing Qualitative Methods).* London: Sage.

Shennan, G. (1998) Are we asking the experts? *Social Work Education*, 17 (4), pp. 407–419.

Sinclair, E.A. (1990) Where Practice Enlightens Theory and Theory Enriches Practice. In Jeffs, T. and Smith M. (eds) *Using Informal Education.* Buckingham: Open University Press.

Smith, M.K. (2001) Chris Argyris: Theories of Action, Double-loop Learning and Organizational Learning, *the Encyclopaedia of Informal Education* (www.infed.org/thinkers/argyris.htm). accessed August 2005.

Smith, R.M. (1984) *Learning How to Learn: Applied Theory for Adults.* Milton Keynes: OU Press.

Smith, C. and White, V. (1997) Parton, Howe and Post Modernity: A Critical Commentary on Mistaken Identity, *British Journal of Social Work*, 27 (2), pp. 275–295.

Social Services Inspectorate (1991) *Getting the Message Across: A Guide to Developing and Communicating Policies, Principles and Procedures on Assessment.* London: HMSO.

Stevenson, O. (2004) The Future of Social Work, Chapter 10. In Lymbery, M. and Butler, S. (eds) *Social Work Ideals and Practice Realities.* Basingstoke: Palgrave Macmillan.

Stevenson, O. (2005) Genericism and Specialisation: The Story since 1970, *British Journal of Social Work*, 35, pp. 569–586.

Taylor, I. (1997) *Developing Learning In Professional Education.* Buckingham: Open University Press/SRHE.

Taylor, I., Thomas, J. and Sage, H. (1999) Portfolios for Learning and Assessment: Laying the Foundations for Continuing Professional Development. *Social Work Education*, 18 (2), pp. 147–159.

Taylor, P. (1993) *The Texts of Paulo Friere.* Buckinghamshire: Open University Press.

Taylor, C. and White, S. (2000) *Practising Reflexivity in Health and Welfare: Making Knowledge.* Buckingham: Open University Press

Taylor, C. and White, S. (2006) Knowledge and Reasoning in Social Work: Educating for Humane Judgement. *British Journal of Social Work*, 36, pp. 937–954.

Tennant, M. (1997) *Psychology and Adult Learning.* London: Routledge.

Thompson, N. (1997) *Anti-Discriminatory Practice.* Basingstoke: Macmillan.

Thompson, N. (2002) *People Skills.* Basingstoke: Palgrave Macmillan.

Thompson, N., Osada, M. and Anderson, B. (1994) *Practice Teaching in Social Work.* Birmingham: Pepar Publications.

Training Organisation for the Personal Social Services UK Partnership (2002) *National Occupational Standards for Social Work.* England: TOPSS.

Urbanowski, M. and Dwyer, M. (1988) *Learning Through Field Instruction: A Guide for Teachers and Students.* Milwaukee: Family Service America.

Vermunt, J.D. (1998) The Regulation of Constructive Learning Processes, *British Journal of Educational Psychology*, 68, pp. 149–171.

Walker, J., McCarthy, P., Morgan, W. and Timms, N. (1995) *In Pursuit of Quality: Improving Practice Teaching in Social Work.* Newcastle upon Tyne: Relate Centre for Family Studies, Newcastle University.

Walter, I., Nutley, S., Percy-Smith, J., McNeish, D. and Frost, S. (2004) Knowledge Review 7 Improving the Use of Research in Social Care Practice. London: SCIE Policy Press.

Welsh Assembly (2006) *Fulfilled Lives*. Supporting Communities Consultation Document. Cardiff: Welsh Assembly Government.

Wilding, P. (2000) *The Welfare State 2000–2050*. A Paper Presented to the Political Studies Association UK Annual Conference, April 2000.

Wilson, S.J. (1980) *Recordings: Guidelines for Social Workers*. New York: Free Press.

Worsley, A. (2003) *Does Age Equal Experience?* National Organisation for Practice Teaching Newsletter, May 2003. NOPT: Stockport.

Worsley, A. (2004) *Probation as Profession*. Unpublished M.Phil. University of Manchester.

Wray, J., Fell, B., Stanley, N., Manthorpe, J. and Coyne, E. (2005) *Best Practice Guide: Disabled Social Work Students and Placements*. Hull: University of Hull

Wright, B. (1989) *Critical Incidents*, Nursing Times 10/05/1989 (www.LSRC.ac.uk) accessed March 2005.

Yelloly, M. and Henkel, M. (eds) *Learning and Teaching in Social Work*. London: Jessica Kingsley Publishers.

Index

Selected Key Authors

Printed and bound by CPI Group (UK) Ltd, Croydon, CR0 4YY